Mascupathy

Understanding and Healing
the Malaise of American Manhood

Charlie Donaldson
Randy Flood

What people say about *Mascupathy*...

Many women in my practice struggle to understand their partner's hurtful, neglectful, and abusive behaviors. I often hear, "I just don't get how he can treat me that way." *Mascupathy* offers the untold story behind men's actions. Women who want to understand men will find in these pages a path towards greater awareness of the root causes of men's behavior – insight that will help them make better decisions about their lives. I welcome this contribution to this very important discussion.
– *Amy Van Gunst, MA, LPC, executive coordinator, Fountain Hill Center for Counseling and Consultation*

Here is the truth from Donaldson and Flood: "Many men go through life believing it's not safe to be fully human." These pioneering cartographers integrate the real-life experience of being a male into a healthy developmental model with pragmatic advice for fostering transformation. More than a window into understanding men, Donaldson and Flood map out a path that will help men to become more fully human.
– *Rev. Dr. Andy Atwood, family business consultant and licensed marriage and family therapist*

It's no secret that many men today are living lives of significant emotional pain and quiet desperation ... evident in violence, broken relationships, mental illness, and chronic health problems. The authors not only offer a clear picture of the core of men's brokenness – the loss of self and soul – they offer a way out ... a wise, detailed roadmap to what it means to be truly male and fully human.
– *Mark Walstrom, co-producer and presenter, "Ideas that Matter: The Fetzer Dialogues"*

Rich with personal stories from men in group treatment, this book offers a clearly presented depiction of males and masculinity. Donaldson and Flood draw on their long careers of working with men to explain the origins of distorted views of masculinity held by many men that result in numb feelings, relationship troubles and, for some, violence. The authors present a group-based treatment that leads to men being freed to be a fuller, richer, version of themselves. Highly recommended for clinicians treating men and for men in their groups, and everyone else!
– *Suzanne Hedstrom, assistant professor, Counselor Education, Counseling Psychology, Western Michigan University*

Flood and Donaldson develop a revolutionary construct: mascupathy. Their approach largely focuses on the amelioration of shame and fear of vulnerability, specific to men. In my work with women and men in relationships and groups, shame is perhaps the most debilitating force in the development of trust and intimacy. Their ideas, therefore, offer hope for all people; boys and men and all of those who live with and love them.
— *Sheila McCormack, Ph.D., licensed clinical psychologist*

As pervasive as body image disturbance is for women, so is mascupathic disorder for men. Both come from an intense cultural pressure to live up to a distorted definition of femininity and masculinity. In *Mascupathy*, Donaldson and Flood describe this narrow definition of masculinity, pointing out that it is a plague on all our houses. Their deep understanding comes from years of clinical experience working with the very men they write about. Thankfully their solutions will not only radically alter the definition of manhood but greatly impact women who will benefit from men who are more liberated and whole.
— *Lavonne Zwart Schaafsma, Psy. D. professor of Human Sexuality and Gender, Calvin College and psychotherapist in private practice*

In this compelling book, Flood and Donaldson name and describe the affliction that has caused so much suffering for men and women for a very long time. Their work provides an invaluable guide for educators, community leaders, advocates, therapists, and indeed for anyone with an interest in the healing of men, which is, of course, all of us. The authors tell us that men do not need to remain locked in destructive patterns of thinking and behaving: both heart and the brain can change. This book is filled with hope.
— *Mark E. DeVries, Ph.D., clinical psychologist, specializing in neuropsychological assessments*

Donaldson and Flood are on to something big. When we look back, taking the long view, we often discover that we were accepting of something "in the water" of our culture, and later it's hard to understand how anyone ever accepted it without question. Why didn't we have a larger vision? That's what the concept of mascupathy is bringing to us, a change of paradigm, a look from outside the bubble.
— *Fanchon M. Clark, MA, LPC, CAADC, family practice therapist*

Mascupathy

Understanding and Healing the Malaise of American Manhood

Charlie Donaldson
Randy Flood

 Institute for the Prevention
& Treatment of Mascupathy
revisioning masculinity | reinventing men

www.mascupathy.org

The Institute for the Prevention and Treatment of Mascupathy
P.O. Box 6010
Grand Rapids, MI 49516-6010
www.mascupathy.org

ISBN: 978-0-615-89891-9
First Edition
Second Printing

Cover Design By: Bultema Lambert Communications
www.bultemalambert.com

We dedicate this book to Bradley J. Ipema
He was what we all seek in ourselves as liberated men,
a model of what it means to love others deeply and hold
space for people, to hear their struggles while sharing his own.
Brad found the balance between work and family,
success and play, congeniality and solitude.
He died too young, having so much left to give.

Preface

Men. We think we know everything about them. We spend our days and lifetimes with them. They are our partners, fathers, sons, and neighbors. We see their competencies – physical strength, loyalty, perseverance. We experience their insufficiencies – rage, distance, and relational ineptness. We take many of their traits and defining qualities for granted.

Yet in many ways we don't fully know men, and they don't know themselves. Many go through life, from the age when they begin to interpret the world around them to the day of their death, reining in the spontaneity and intimacy of childhood, believing it's not safe to be fully human.

Men often secret away enough of themselves that they can't be completely understood: their joy or darkness, what they cherish, or the fear of shame that too often rules their lives. When their unconscious suffering consequently explodes, it sends painful shards everywhere: on a personal level, from frustrating relationships to premature death; on a societal level, from domestic violence to mass shootings.

In this time of seismic change in gender roles, men's struggles have intensified as women increasingly take their rightful place in the world and as economies shift and a new consciousness emerges. Many are unable to meet the challenges this new day presents. Not only do they face the dilemma that traditional masculine behaviors have become both less acceptable and functional, they also find themselves wary of new gender roles, clinging stubbornly to the mores of their fathers who they saw as "the man of the house."

This book offers new ideas as to why men behave the way they do. But it's more than an exploration of men's psyches. It's also the story of how we, as both men and therapists, came to understand men's ongoing struggle with masculinity and how to best treat them.

Our journey began with the recognition that conventional theories and approaches to treating men frequently failed because they didn't emphasize the issues that brought men to therapy: fear, shame, and loneliness. The journey continued with insights from feminists, who were breaking down stereotypes of femininity, and with the perceptions of other male therapists and academicians who were exploring new gender roles for men.

Recognizing that the real origins of men's bad behavior were not the inherently flawed psyches of men so much as the socialization that rules men's lives, we developed a new diagnosis, mascupathy, for what ailed men, and created targeted therapies that enabled substantial client progress. Finally, we realized that therapy alone would not bring a wide-spread alteration in men and manhood, and so we explored societal programs that change men as individuals as well as the culture they inhabit.

The accounts of the struggles and personal growth of men in this book come from our clinical practices, focus groups, and from our own lives. Some are amalgams of various clients. In some cases, we've changed names and circumstances to protect client confidentially. Our personal stories are factual.

One more thing: As we wrote this book, we were influenced by experiences beyond our clinical practices. We have always been aware that the history of the human race is a chronicle of great progress diminished by episodes of extreme violence. But after viewing the graphic and painful film *12 Years a Slave*, and traveling abroad, where we learned more about the mayhem and massacres in the history of other cultures, we were reminded that mascupathy is as old as the human race and as new as the recent mass shootings in our cities and the bombings in Baghdad. In a sense, it has always been with us. Now is as good a time as any – perhaps better – for a change.

As our practices have given us hope, we see optimism on a societal level as well. This is a time of new consciousness for people across our nation: the new generation seems to be increasingly accepting of differences, rejecting of hierarchy, and open to a new sense of community. There is hope, and this book is about that hope. Our desire is that it opens new doors to more fulfilling lives for both men and women.

Table of Contents

PART I: Presenting Problems

Early on in our clinical practices, it became clear that most male clients struggled with disorders beyond depression or PTSD. They frequently exhibited guardedness and insularity rooted in the belief that it's not safe to be fully human, and their denial of the elemental need for intimate belonging had literally made them sick. Conventional treatments often proved ineffective. Benefitting from the work of feminists and from gender role studies, we developed a new vision of masculinity that gave reason for hope.

Facing up to the tough reality of American manhood

Beyond conventional descriptors of men and masculinity

Unexpected awakenings from men in deep sleep

PART II: Origins of Tough Guys and Disappointing Partners

While some observers cite genes as the problem in male misbehavior, the men in our practices appeared warped by male socialization, resulting in anxiety and acting-out behaviors. Born with a love for spontaneity and intimacy, boys were frequently shamed out of playfulness into invulnerability and distance. As men, they were often admirable, but their closeted angst and anger conspired to undermine their better natures.

Strictures of socialization that steal boys' spirits and innocent psyches

Chapter 5: Hidden Feelings that Deaden Men's Souls   65
Unseen events and forces that rule men's lives

PART III: New Directions
Men in conventional therapies frequently remained incapacitated. We found a fresh model for understanding masculinity and a new name for the malaise of manhood that not only clarified men's problems but also provided new directions for treatment.

Chapter 6: A Pathology of Masculinity   83
A diagnosis that provides understanding rather than demonization of men

Chapter 7: Varieties of Mascupathy   91
Men with similar roots but diverse symptoms

Part IV: Healing
New forms of therapy in our practices started with resocialization groups that replace distorted belief systems with self-disclosure and empathy. Recognizing that accountability training could ameliorate abusive behavior but not enlarge the capacity for open-hearted relationships, we introduced interactive treatments which exhorted men to explore their psyches in a challenging but safe group setting where they moved beyond resentful self-interest to a new sense of community.

Chapter 8: Resocialization Training   105
The academy of undoing mascupathic beliefs and supplanting them with accountable thinking and behavior

Chapter 9: Reclamation and Recovery   115
An initial wariness of male group therapy that disappears as men make life-changing forays into their psyches

Chapter 10: Societal Change toward a New Masculinity   129
Individuals/societal institutions now asserting a new masculinity in surprising and hopeful ways

Epilogue   145
Resources   151
Acknowledgements   155
About the Authors   157

Foreword

Men working on the transformation of conventional masculinity in recent decades have steadily made progress in three areas: assisting boys to succeed on the journey to manhood, coaching men to become better fathers and father figures, and teaching men who are violent how to stop their abusive behavior. Concurrently, some psychologists, psychotherapists, and counselors have been working on a fourth area – treating men so they can open their hearts as well as their minds. For more than a quarter century, therapists Charlie Donaldson and Randy Flood have staked out the territory of men's inner lives as the place to apply their ample shoulders to the wheel of change – helping men grow from the inside out.

Their early clients were men struggling to overcome substance abuse addictions and/or who were still acting abusively in their intimate relationships. While Donaldson and Flood each focused on treating individual men as well as facilitating men's therapy groups, they never lost sight of the bigger picture, locating their work inside of the social justice, profeminist wing of the men's movement.

Having identified the limitations of cognitive behavioral therapy in working with men – a methodology that favors changing men's thoughts and actions – they began searching for a more nuanced and emotionally deep therapeutic model. They concluded that any approach that didn't seek to deconstruct male socialization – beginning with the damaging messages males receive as babies and little boys (what boy hasn't heard the phrase "Big boys don't cry?") – would fall short at treating the underlying turmoil their clients were experiencing.

Who can deny that male socialization works to silence men, shaming them from even questioning their isolation and disconnection as well as undermining their latent yearnings to roam the expansive region of the heart? Donaldson and Flood became convinced there had to be a way to connect men with their hearts. When they realized there were no existing treatment modalities that worked both to deconstruct male socialization *and* integrate men's hearts and heads, they set out to create one. In *Mascupathy: Understanding and Healing the Malaise of American Manhood,* they lay out their hopeful conclusions.

Nearly a half-century ago female psychologists, in response to women's disadvantaged position in society because of their gender, developed what became known as feminist psychotherapy. Flood's and Donaldson's explanation of mascupathy now provides a high-powered lens for therapists – and others – with which to examine *how men experience their own disadvantaged position in society* because of *their* gender.

Before she wrote *The Feminine Mystique,* Betty Friedan described the state of women as being "a problem with no name." By contrast, the state of men is a problem that has long had a name – a few, in fact – male privilege, entitlement, and patriarchy. In developing their ideas about mascupathy, the authors have disassembled the aspects of masculinity that emphasize power and control what is normally in the spotlight – while strengthening the spiritual and emotional components too often found in the shadows.

Extremists in the men's rights movement might deny the overwhelming concentration of power men still hold in a patriarchal society. Even they, however, cannot deny that the insularity, loneliness, and false sense of autonomy most men live with are the toxic byproducts of mascupathy. And, just as women over the last half-century have made tremendous strides in moving from oppression to empowerment (there certainly remains much to be done), men today are moving from a limited emotional vocabulary to more fluently being able to speak "Emotionalese" and, at the same time, joining with their life-partners in authentic and intimate bonds.

16

Over the course of their careers, Donaldson and Flood have worked hard to grow personally, not just facilitating men's groups but participating in long-running ones they have held close to their hearts. Beyond that, they have used their own histories to untangle the malaise of contemporary manhood rather than simply dispassionately explaining mascupathy. They disclose stories from their boyhoods, inviting readers to see the impact that growing up male has had on *them*. By deeply sharing painful, personal anecdotes alongside expert analysis, they model a healthy masculinity. Other men, writing a book like this, might have consciously decided to maintain a professional distance, leaving the reader to wonder about the author's own experiences as a male in this society. In writing with such openness and vulnerability, Donaldson and Flood are walking their talk. *Mascupathy* offers men – and the women in their lives – a new tack to a safe harbor where they can be both empowered and free.

Rob Okun
Author, *VOICE MALE: The Untold Story of the Profeminist Men's Movement*
Editor, *Voice Male* magazine

Introduction

In 2012, then New Jersey mayor, Cory Booker, ran into a burning home against his security team's wishes and saved a young woman's life. In January 2009, pilot Chesley "Sully" Sullenberger, III successfully landed US Airways Flight 1549 in the Hudson River off Manhattan after the plane was disabled by striking a flock of Canada geese as it departed LaGuardia Airport. All 155 passengers and crew aboard the aircraft survived. A lifetime away, Oskar Schindler, a German businessman (and subject of the Academy Award-winning movie, *Schindler's List*) risked his life saving the lives of more than a thousand Jews during the Holocaust by employing them in his factories. We have all heard stories of men who do honorable and noble things, and we probably know heroic men whose actions – large or small – haven't made the news.

Still, in day-to-day life, it's hard to ignore the disturbing things men do. A sunny Sunday afternoon baseball game turns into fisticuffs. A wannabe partygoer opens fire on those who didn't include him. A football player bullies a fellow team member. A simple display of affection suddenly morphs into unwelcome sex. The media is full of such stories.

Regular guys. It's a commonplace remark that "men behave badly," and since they often don't talk about what's behind their behavior it's easy to assume the worst. Yet, as therapists, we've observed that the vast majority of men do not act with malice. Very few, in fact, are sociopathic. They're just "regular guys."

When you look behind the mask, it's clear that most men's proclivity for criticism, derision, and abuse does not stem from impatience, self-interest, or even the desire to harm another person, but more from a pervasive insecurity that if things are not done right, the center will not hold. Or more accurately, *their* center will not hold. What we have observed is that men frequently act out of a secret panic that danger is all around them and that it must always be kept at bay.

Years of experience taught us to look to men's insecurities as a reason for their bad behavior. We found validation for our ideas in the work of feminist psychologist Harriet Lerner, author of *The Dance of Intimacy*, who observed:

> It's said men remain silent because they want to exert power over women.... [Actually] men choose not to talk because they don't know how to make themselves heard, because they believe that problems get worse when you talk about them, because they dread conflict and criticism, or because they feel trapped in a conversation that feels awful.

Lerner's statement clearly and succinctly describes men's experience, but it doesn't address what it is that causes men to believe and act the way they do or where these fundamental feelings of distrust come from. We discovered that the adult men with whom we worked had stored away powerful life lessons – learned most often from other men – that led to interpersonal problems. We heard hundreds of stories from men who shared tragic experiences of fathers teaching their sons the importance of toughness and vigilance. Here's an account from Ross, who had been in the men's therapy group almost a year when he shared this story about a lesson his father taught him.

> *I was five or six years old, and I was playing on the top bunk of the bed I shared with my brother. I had the top, he had the bottom. My dad came into the bedroom and told me to jump off the bed into his arms. I was scared to jump that far, I was scared that my dad wouldn't catch me. Well, my dad said, "Come on, come on, I won't drop you, just jump." So I finally mustered the courage and pushed off from the bunk. At the last moment, my dad dropped his arms and I fell on the floor. He just stood there as I starting crying, "Daddy, why didn't you catch me?" He said, "Don't trust anybody, Ross. You got to watch out. There are always guys out there who'll try to get you."*

New nomenclature. Unfortunately, Ross's account was typical of the many guys in our practices – both self-referred and court-referred – for whom socialization from parents, coaches, and teachers so bruised their healthy psyches that they became broken men. In our clinical experience, conventional American male socialization leads to an excess of masculine energy and repression of feminine traits resulting in inadequate emotional literacy and poor relational skills. Harboring these deficits is painful and can cause men to externalize (act out) behaviors that negatively impact their own lives and their primary relationships.

We have worked with men of all races, origins, and socio-economic backgrounds: CEOs, drywallers, teachers, managers, plumbers, attorneys, and the homeless. No matter their differences, their psyches are remarkably similar: most suffer from a distortion of a natural masculinity. We developed the term "mascupathy," a pathology (sickness) of masculinity, to describe the pattern of thinking and behavior that we repeatedly observed in the men in our treatment programs. Although our insights are gathered from an anecdotal clinical sample, we observe and postulate that many men, even though they may not walk through the doors of a counseling office, also suffer from a similar malaise.

Our criteria establish mascupathy as an illness similar to other psychiatric disorders. While its symptoms have presented themselves in men for centuries, we believe mascupathy has gone unrecognized as a separate pathology because its symptoms have simply been accepted as normal behavior. Mascupathy's commonality makes the pathology seem normal to men and women alike – like the water in which fish swim or the air humans breathe.

Our purpose in developing the concept of mascupathy is not to demonize men but to facilitate an understanding so they aren't demonized. We believe understanding men's unhealthy behavior as stemming from a disorder of the psyche and not an inherent orientation toward malevolence will lead to greater insight and compassion.

Alcoholics Anonymous (A.A.) founder Bill Wilson performed a great service when he popularized the disease concept of alcoholism. Just as the term "alcoholic" no longer automatically conjures images of depravity, mascupathy need not denigrate men. Beyond removing alcoholism from the realm of character flaw, Wilson also advocated accountability. In the A.A. "Big Book" he clearly expects alcoholics to admit they have an illness and to seek help for it. In the same way, those suffering from various forms of mascupathy need to acknowledge their disorder and take steps to heal themselves from it.

Defining the logic behind mascupathy. While human behavior may often seem perplexing, there's always logic behind it. In the case of male behavior, there's the "man-pact" and the "man-pack." Though unwritten and seldom spoken of, the man-pact could be considered the most influential doctrine of all time. A code of conduct that demands toughness and invulnerability, it lays out dark principles about men's relationships to others. Chief among them is a strict adherence to male hierarchy including subjugation of and dominance over those perceived as inadequate and different.

The man-pact is a convoluted but systematic set of instructions that all men, to one degree or another, live by. Meanwhile, the man-pact is enforced by the man-pack, which may be the largest collective in the world. Every man consciously or unconsciously belongs to the man-pack and organizes most of his beliefs and behaviors around membership in the pack. Here's Mitch's account of his struggle to meet the requirements of the man-pact.

My wife died suddenly. Really suddenly. I couldn't believe it. She was alive one day and gone the next. After a couple weeks, I went back to work. At the place I work, it's all men; all my bosses are men. There's a couple of female secretaries, but that's it. They all say they're sorry, and I say, "Thank you," but I don't know what else to say. I'm really struggling, but I can't go in and tell everybody what's going on with me without having a breakdown, and I really don't want to do that.

After a while, I'm not getting along with people very well. Everything just keeps on getting more uncomfortable for me. So I start not showing up for work, and I just hang out in my apartment, remembering the good times JoAnne and I had together. But that just gets me depressed, and finally I decided I had to do something, so that's why I'm here in this group.

What Mitch needs to do, of course, is to just talk about his feelings, which is precisely what the man-pact commands him not to do.

A structure for treatment. Feminism is a model for much of our work, especially in that it recognized that traditional therapies were inadequate and ill-chosen for oppressed women. In developing a structure for the diagnosis and treatment of mascupathy – which recognizes that men, too, are oppressed albeit in a different way – we relied upon the larger exploration of gender roles over the last half-century which provided insight and regimens for treatment.

The concept of mascupathy transforms traditional treatment by focusing on symptoms we have long observed in most of our clients, rather than on those listed in the American Psychiatric Association's *Diagnostic and Statistical Manual of Mental Disorders (DSM)*. Conventional views of the origin of men's psychological problems assume that men suffer from basic mental health disorders – anxiety, depression, addiction – and that these issues lead to relationship problems. We think the "conventional view" has it backwards. Using the frame of mascupathy reveals the opposite: men's unsatisfying relationships – or lack of relationships at all – produce loneliness and alienation, and it is these feelings that generate depression, anxiety, acting-out behaviors such as addiction and classic withdrawal. Here's an example:

> *Jackie and Jesse had been married for 10 years, and Jackie's great frustration was Jesse's unwillingness to participate in her family outings. Sometimes she assumed he was simply depressed, when the fact was he found her family's teasing and joviality so intimidating that he would withdraw. He saw his attempts at humor as off-key and unfunny – no one laughed at his jokes and over time he felt humiliated by his inability to take part in the fun.*

It is fear of further shame that kept Jesse away. In Jesse's view of things, admitting it would only expose him to more shame. Jesse was not depressed or a bad guy, but like many men, he planned his life around the avoidance of shame.

Change. Most guys are more similar to Jesse than to a sociopath; they're neither hateful nor violent, but they struggle with the basic aspects of genuine relationships: affection, affirmation, self-disclosure, expression of feelings. It may be tempting to say, "Men aren't going to change. It's just the way they are." We don't accept that defeatist narrative.

Psychiatrist and author Frank Pittman observed, "The male chorus demands that men honor their masculinity before they consider comfort, their humanity, their soul, and that of others." When men are trained to listen to enlightened voices and offered a hand to access qualities that open them to the fullness of their humanity, they learn to extend themselves beyond the confines of rigid masculinity. We have found that once men stop depriving themselves of human connection and instead form authentic relationships with other people, their conventional presenting problems often disappear. This change in awareness is often facilitated in men's Resocialization Training and Experiential Reclamation Therapy groups – experiences that most men will carry with them the rest of their lives.

Because our expertise is men and their psychology, there are several areas that this book doesn't cover:

- Throughout this book, we speak of the assault of male gender socialization on men. We recognize that women also face similar issues with their socialization.
- Our observations in this book are written for men of all races, ethnic, and socio-economic groups, as well as from many walks of life. While there are certainly variations which we do not have expertise to expound upon, we believe our conclusions are frequently universal and neither exclude nor are exclusive to any group. Though written primarily about heterosexual men, we anticipate its ideas will be useful to gay, bisexual, and transgendered people as well.
- We are convinced that some of the most egregious aspects of mascupathy are the subjugation and decimation by some groups of American men of various other societal groups: women, Native

Americans, African-Americans, and ethnic minorities. When mixed with racism, the emasculation of other races is even more vile, causing further suffering of men and the destruction of families. We see homophobia as a symptom of mascupathy, and decry the physical and emotional abuse it promotes of GLBT people. These issues, however, are primarily in the realm of sociology and not addressed in this book.

- There is need for a separate book about the implications of mascupathy for women, Native Americans, African-Americans, and ethnic groups. Though we surmise that our ideas pertain to men of non-U.S. nationalities, we haven't worked with enough international clients to adequately verify the appropriateness of our conclusions.

Revisioning masculinity, reinventing men. The last half-century saw revolutionary change for women as they moved from the kitchen to the boardroom. We believe that the upcoming decades of this century will constitute a new era for men, one where conventional masculinity ends and an awakening among men takes root. Though many men struggle, others are moving forward in this journey as they find the other half of their humanity. We hope you'll see the transformation of men as ushering in a new order, one that ameliorates abuse and violence while enriching both society at large and human relationships.

PART I

Presenting Problems

1

The Malaise of Men

In September 2013, Aaron Alexis shot and killed a dozen people at the Washington Navy Shipyard. The previous year, there were seven horrific shootings perpetrated by seven lone killers: Andrew Engeldinger, Wade Michael Page, Ian Stawicki, One L. Goh, James Holmes, Jeong Soo Paek, and Adam Lanza. After each mass shooting, the national conversation focused on gun control, the murderers' mental health problems, the role of the Internet and, sometimes, extreme religious beliefs. These are all important issues, but there's something missing from the conversation. Something else that demands attention.

What did the shooters have in common? Many may have been diagnosed as mentally ill. They may have shared an interest in weapons and/or violent video games. *What is most obvious and indisputable is: the shooters were all men.* In fact, according to *Mother Jones* magazine, in the 31 years between 1982 and 2013, 66 of 67 mass shooters were men.

Tens of millions of women are diagnosed with mental illness, and a good many of them like guns, but in the last 30 years only one has become a mass shooter. What's going on with the men who shoot and maim innocent people? Why, according to the Centers for Disease Control (CDC), are an estimated 1.3 million women victims of physical assault by an intimate partner – usually male – each year? And why do men in the United States, as Will Courtenay writes in *Dying to be Men*, engage in more risky behaviors, suffer greater numbers of preventable health conditions, and die more than five years earlier than women? Beyond what they do to each other, women, and children, men struggle with their own psyches. CDC statistics report that they kill themselves *four times* more frequently than do women. Why is there seemingly a conversation about everything else but men and masculinity?

For years we have asked ourselves: why do concerned and thoughtful men and women overlook the reality of male violence? Probably because the pervasiveness of male aggression reinforces the social narrative that men will behave badly. The result? Pundits, government officials, the media, and the general public unwittingly all collude to accept men's violence in a grand version of "boys will be boys." Instead of being viewed along the lines of epidemics and viral outbreaks, which can be treated, men's acts of mayhem are reported in the same manner as hurricanes and tornados – inherent in the nature of things.

A touchstone for a greater malaise. We cite the gender of the shooters because it is a bellwether for the more common problems of contemporary American manhood. What we have discovered in our years working with a wide range of men is this: many aspects of their lives influence their thinking, feelings, and behavior including genetic make-up, family of origin trauma, and cultural and economic backgrounds. The one common factor is the role of masculinity – in particular, the socialized drive that virtually all men share to be tough enough, stoic enough, strong enough, *man enough*.

As different as shooters are from "regular guys," their similarity lies in their exposure to male socialization; their difference lies in their response to that exposure. While there is no doubt some men who come into schools, mosques, and movie theaters to shoot are sociopaths, often they're also men whose shame and self-contempt for not being adequately masculine enough is all-consuming. Typically, they have been repeatedly bullied or marginalized by other men, and their obsession with proving their masculinity morphs into compulsive and misplaced retaliation perpetrated on both bullies and innocent bystanders.

In the act of killing, they see themselves becoming the quintessential macho man who takes no prisoners. They replicate

30

the image of the strong, tough guy – a "winner" portrayed in movies and video games striding triumphantly across a field of bombed-out buildings and bodies.

The rest of us. As therapists, we see people with psychiatric disorders as differing in degree, not kind. Most guys do not struggle with physical violence towards others, but their hearts are often lacking in empathy and their minds are filled with self-recrimination and the shame of inadequate manhood. In spite of their struggles, they can be good companions, sometimes fun to be around, great in a crisis, and generally do the right thing. But most of the time they aren't authentic, and can be disappointing and exhausting to live with. For many men, there's a fundamental incongruence between the sad and mad man inside and the inconsistent charm he exhibits in order to be accepted. Some men allay their inner struggles with compulsive use of alcohol, sex, and work. Most men manage the discrepancy in more socially acceptable ways. However – like Harold in the following account - their self-assumed inadequacy can weigh upon them and induce a malaise that distances them from loved ones and the joys of life.

Harold was a tenured professor of American History at one of the schools in the University of California system. He grew up on a small farm in northern New England. In an interview with his therapist, Rob, Harold said that he knew he was different from the start: he read books when the other kids were learning to fix cars; he hung out with his sisters to avoid a father who was often furious with him because he couldn't hammer a nail straight. A big kid, he got beat up by smaller guys at school because he didn't fight back. "I just never fit in," he said. "Never man enough?" Rob asked. Harold looked him in the eye: "You got that right."

In high school things got a little better. Because of his size, Harold was a star on the football team. He learned to hunt with other guys. In college, he joined ROTC and earned respect for his sense of discipline and the ability to command other men. "Three entrées into the male world," he said.

Over the years, Harold got a Ph.D., became widely known for his expertise on the Civil War, and wrote four textbooks for history classes that are still in wide use. He and his attractive

31

wife bought a lovely old rambling home north of San Francisco with room for their children and grandchildren to spend idyllic summers.

He was president of the home owners' association and ran marathons.

Harold was a success by any standard. Yet, he told Rob, "Sometimes I still feel like an outsider. I get in a group of men, and I don't know the language. I don't banter like they do. It's not because I'm shy. It's because I'm different, and they know it." Harold closed his eyes and put his huge hand on his forehead. "It's better. I mean, I'm better than I've been most of my life, but I'll never be one of them."

"Listen to me, Harold," Rob responded, "You know yourself really well. But you don't know them. Most of them, Harold, feel as lonely and estranged as you do."

"Rob," Harold said, "I'll never believe that."

For virtually all men, there is no escaping mascupathy. Unlike many guys, Harold did not act out – he was neither abusive nor addictive. But even though he understood the roots of his malaise better than most, he still could not shake off its effects. Despite his best intentions and efforts to be a good man, his darkness cast a shadow over his wife and family, those whom he most wanted to make happy.

Harold was a relatively open man. He spoke frankly to his therapist about his struggle with his masculinity. Steve Biddulph, author of *Manhood*, speaks for many other men who have drawn the curtain to hide the extreme discomfort of their inner lives.

> Most men don't have a life. Instead we have an act, an outer show, kept up for protection. We pretend things are fine, that everything is cool, and sometimes we even fool ourselves. But ask a man how he really feels or what he really thinks, the first thing he thinks is 'what am I supposed to say?' The average man today is deeply unhappy but he would be the last to admit it.

> Most women are not like this. Women today act from inner feelings and spirits, and more and more they know who they are and what they want. The Women's Movement

helped this along, but women were always more in touch with themselves and each other. The men in relationships with these strong, healthy women were no match for them, in every sense of that word. Conversations go nowhere, relationships collapse; because to be in a relationship, you have to first know who you are.

A wake up call. We write about male shooters not because they have much in common with ordinary American men – they don't – but because shooters are our wake-up call. As murderers, they are the most extreme example of what happens when a man's struggle to be "man enough" fails. Unwittingly perhaps, they invite, no, *demand*, we pay attention to the role of masculinity and male socialization in American society.

Shooters are like the canary in the coal mine warning us to pay attention, to dig deeper in our efforts at understanding men. For example:

- Why do two men aggressively jockey for pole position as the road narrows and then dangerously try to out maneuver one another on down the highway?
- Why does a guy diagnosed with cancer refrain from telling anybody about his condition and demand that his wife follow suit?
- Why, if you ask a man what he's feeling, does he just continue with the story, oblivious to its emotional component?
- Why do college buddies who get together after 20 years ignore two decades of touching stories of triumph and disappointment only to spend an evening in hollow banter?

Men can change. We live in an age that cherishes personal transformation. Popular culture is replete with stories of reinvention and resocialization: juvenile delinquents turn into good citizens, sinners are reborn, and bigots renounce their hateful attitudes.

Beyond the failure to see that the problem of men is their distorted masculinity, the possibility of rehabilitation is generally ignored. The assumption that the psyche of the male persona is intractable has been rigidly embedded in our national consciousness. But we know that men can and do change. We've seen them do it. They develop an egalitarian view of women in the workforce and an acceptance of gays and lesbians. Guys in Bible study begin the group wanting only to speak of scripture, but graduate into healing self-disclosure. Men attend treatment groups out of desperation and considerable skepticism, yet transform from angry and lonely guys into accountable and emotionally available human beings.

Carlos, a middle-aged man who had fought with feelings of inadequacy and measured his days in degrees of self-recrimination, wrote this about his path to a better life:

> *It was in hearing men in group therapy talk about their experiences of being ostracized, intimidated, and disdained – as well as admitting their own acts of ostracism, persecution, and disdain – that I discovered I was not a pariah: I was not the only one.*

> *I witnessed these guys – for whom I had gained great respect – wince with humiliation as they described shaming situations with their parents, wives, kids, coworkers. Gradually it came to me that these dark feelings didn't control their lives, because when they told their stories, and other men nodded their heads with compassion, the heavy weight they were carrying lifted.*

> *So I began speaking about what I was carrying – my pain – and I found that when they had compassion for me, I could, amazingly, have compassion for myself. Slowly, over many years and in various groups with a variety of men, I healed.*

As we strive to understand the struggle of Carlos and other men here are seven key observations that inform our perspective on masculinity:

1. Although we recognize the role genetics plays in male disposition, we believe the forces of socialization, not the inherent character of men themselves, are responsible for men not accessing the relational aspects of the feminine while exacerbating the insularity of the masculine.
2. Though outside forces are powerful, men can change and must be responsible for their behavior.

34

3. Virtually all men struggle with their sense of manhood, dealing with loneliness, fear, and shame. While a minority of men are violent, the majority of others are, in the view of many women at least, relationally inadequate.

4. Some males subjugate women and emasculate men who they deem "different," oblivious to the stark truth that they are also the victims of their own oppression.

5. Men need not abandon traditional masculine values such as competitiveness, leadership, and physicality but they can benefit from acquiring values customarily associated with the feminine – collaboration, cooperation, nurturing – to achieve a more balanced humanity.

6. Some forms of male aggression are shame-based, reactive, and destructive manifestations of an exaggerated masculinity. Other forms of aggression – used with discernment to protect self and family – exemplify a more developed and healthy masculinity.

7. More men are working to transform themselves through treatment, and society is responding by amending its values to help foster new definitions of manhood. Many men are remarkably willing to disclose personal matters with other men in safe social environments such as therapy groups.

In summary, we believe that the majority of men are good guys. We write about their limitations – their dark side – to explain the struggle of masculinity. We describe their inner brawls and their daily skirmishes with other men and women because we believe that most men are inadequately aware of their psyches and restricted in their relationships, and because we are convinced that understanding will bring change.

2

A New Template

Like many psychotherapists, we began our counseling practices treating major depression and bipolar disorders using insight and cognitive-behavioral therapy. But as we listened to the stories of men's lives, we realized we heard more about fear than depression, shame than mood disorders, and loneliness than delusion. We realized we needed something more than could be found in the diagnoses of the *DSM*.

Mark's story is one such example. He had been in the group for eight months and had frequently spoken of the trauma of growing up with his father, a police officer, who abhorred signs of weakness, particularly the tears of a young boy. Mark told this story:

> *At the age of eight, after he had cried one day, his father handcuffed Mark to the mailbox with a bath towel tied around him like a diaper so the kids in the neighborhood could see "the baby."*

> *Mark described his humiliation from this event on the day of Jacob's first session. New to the group, Jacob was stunned. He couldn't imagine disclosing such intimate matters and didn't think he'd ever do that.*

> *Yet a couple months later, more acclimated to the group than he knew, Jacob shared how his father had once abandoned him at night in the woods to teach him not to be afraid of the dark. Jacob said the lesson sort of worked: he confessed that he'd lived*

his whole life pretending that he was never afraid, and also knowing he didn't hide his fear well.

The *DSM* serves up a banquet of intriguing disorders that describe a range of aberrations from the norm. Yet when it comes to males, it neglects the fundamental domains of men's experience, especially men like Jacob and Mark. Their dads' cruel treatment did not result in panic attacks or conventional depression. Rather, they struggled with knee-jerk defensiveness and harbored a protective insularity that led to pervasive loneliness. We realized that if we wanted to explain the behavior of men like Mark and Jacob and find ways to help them, we needed to think differently about them.

Therapists talk about the "big three" dark emotions: hurt, fear, and shame. Most agree that hurt really isn't in a class with the other two. Fear and shame are more searing and have greater staying power.

Both men and women live in fear of humiliation. Often the teaching moments are mortifying and, like those experienced by Mark and Jacob, leave permanent damage that emerges as shame in adulthood. Other times they subversively influence similar situations in the brain. For example, Jacob feigning a smile as the doctor tells him he has brain cancer while his grown children look on. Men have their own singular socialized stigmas. Mark and Jacob's fathers and other role models – teachers, coaches, and celebrities – set them up to:

- Live with few feelings – *emotions are unmanly, feminine*
- Keep distant from others – *don't get too close, especially with other men, or people might think you're gay*
- Experience persistent loneliness - *it's safer to keep a distance*
- Exaggerate autonomy – *asking for help invites mockery*
- Act right – *watch out, if you say or do the wrong thing, you'll be ridiculed and shamed*
- Stay in control – *vulnerability exposes you to more hurt and shame.*

A New Look

In our search for a more powerful lens through which we might see men more clearly, we looked to the literature of gender role socialization – the process of inculcating children with societal norms and values.

Close to a half century ago, feminists began revolutionizing our understanding of gender, demonstrating that gender roles were not inherent but social constructs. They brought the dark side of gender role stereotypes to light, focusing on the inclusion of men and the exclusion of women. As Carol Gilligan pointed out in her catalytic book, *In a Different Voice*, traditional psychology had ignored the voices and experiences of women, having based its research only on white male participants. In so doing, it replicated society's deprivation and marginalization of women. And Betty Friedan, in her groundbreaking book *The Feminine Mystique*, challenged the narrow definition of women's roles, in particular taking Freud to task for his contention that, "Law and custom have much to give women that has been withheld from them, but the position of women will surely be what it is: in youth an adored darling and in mature years a loved wife."

Following in the footsteps of these leading women, male psychologists began writing about their male clients as well as their own experiences. Over the last 40 years, they contributed revolutionary ideas that challenged accepted views of masculinity. Two pioneers, Paul Kivel in *Men's Work* and Frank Pittman in *Man Enough*, exposed the systemic social structure that induces and coerces boys to sacrifice a big part of their humanity in service to a man's toughness, domination, and power. In his documentary, *Tough Guise 2: Violence, Media and the Crisis in Masculinity*, educator-activist Jackson Katz revealed how hyper-masculine media images encourage men to mask their fear and shame. And therapist Terry Real challenged traditional concepts of men's mental health in *I Don't Want to Talk About It*, describing the covert depression that men won't admit they experience.

Men's Struggles Go Unnamed

Just as Friedan once described the state of women as "a problem with no name," in our work with men, we realized that the malaise men experience was also nameless. We recognized that the *DSM* offered no overarching concept, no identifying moniker for therapists to understand male clients and plan their therapies.

Early in our practices, when we worked primarily with men who had abused women, we'd often describe batterers as "hyper-masculine." As we broadened our practices to include a range of men, we realized that the term "hyper-masculine" only represented some men. Many of our clients did not manifest aggression and toughness; they were *hypo*-masculine: unable or unwilling to meet the taxing requirements of masculinity, nonetheless acting out like other men but for different reasons. We also encountered men who fit neither the definition of "hyper-" or "hypo-" masculine, whose characteristics fell along the continuum. Some, for instance, experienced chronic patterns of mood fluctuation, impulsive behavior, and intermittent, high levels of anxiety about their masculinity while others, although otherwise well-adjusted, had difficulty engaging in intimate relationships.

Degrees of Mascupathy

We believe that the presence of mascupathy causes impairment in four domains of human functioning: self-concept, emotionality, relationships, and behavior.

- **Weak self-concept** – A deficient or distorted (i.e., grandiose) sense of self, creating incongruence between thoughts/feelings and actions, resulting in withdrawal and insularity or impulsive and aggressive behavior

- **Inadequate emotionality** – Difficulty with experiencing, naming, managing, expressing, and governing feelings leading to behavioral instability and shallow and/or conflictive relationships

- **Relational deficits** – A pattern of interpersonal controlling, distancing, and/or needy behaviors resulting in reduced capacity to establish and maintain satisfying, intimate, and enduring relationships

- **Externalization** – A proclivity for engagement in acting-out behaviors such as addictions to substances, work, and sex; aggression towards partners and family; planned or random acts of violence such as mass shootings or genocide to relieve unresolved feelings of fear, shame, and loneliness, and in compensation for the feeling of "not being man enough."

The severity of mascupathy ranges from severe to moderate to mild. Some men are rage-filled and violent while others fall prey to anger and abuse. A few escape externalization and are almost always respectful and compassionate.

The severe form of mascupathy we call "consuming" because, like an addiction, it takes over, leaving no aspect of life unaffected. "Problematic," the moderate form, refers to the mascupath who displays fewer symptoms but, similar to a problem-drinker, has a disorder that manifests in some behavioral and relational difficulties. The "negligible" mascupath is comparatively symptom-free, but nevertheless struggles with occasional distorted thinking and errant behavior.

Domains of Human Functioning	Consuming (Severe)
Self-concept	Weak and unstable self-concept leading to rigid patriarchal and grandiose thinking and aggressive/ intimidating and sociopathic behavior including hyper-competitiveness and violence or asocial insularity and alienation
Emotionality	A poverty of healthy emotionality including the inability to identify, name, experience, express, or govern feelings; profound sense of failure, inability to empathize or express compassion
Relationships	Poor, unstable relationships with frequent conflicts resulting in excessive and abusive behaviors; virtually no self-disclosure or intimacy, often resulting in an obsession with sex as a substitute for emotional connection
Externalization	Frequent externalization (acting out) with inadequate accountability through addictions, excessive work, sex, violence, and high-risk activities, compensating for frustrations resulting from limited life skills, especially deficits in relationships

Problematic (Moderate)	Negligible (Mild)
Variable self-concept resulting in moderate interference with human functioning; hierarchical thinking, excessive need for control, aggressiveness or episodic withdrawal	Stable, balanced, and positive self-concept with generally respectful and egalitarian thinking; occasional self-aggrandizing and controlling behavior, especially during times of stress
Limited or inconsistent emotional awareness; moderate deficiency in managing and expressing feelings; restricted capacity to empathize	Consistent ability to name, experience, express, and govern feelings; frequent positive emotionality with moderate to high capacity for empathy; occasional emotional distancing and/or over-reaction
Shifting levels of satisfaction with partners and friends; moderate and variable levels of openness and intimacy; conflict resolution skills reduced in times of stress	Responsive, caring, and respectful with partners and friends; generally able to self-disclose, express empathy and enter into intimacy; occasional mild acts of aggression or withdrawal
Moderate levels of externalization as a result of conflicts in relationships, disappointment or stress; limited accountability as demonstrated through episodic rationalization and blaming	Generally high levels of accountability and limited use of externalizing behaviors due to relatively accurate and balanced perceptions of self and others

Here's the story of Gerald, who attended a men's therapy group and exhibited signs of a problematic/moderate mascupath.

Retired from the armed services, Gerald displayed mascupathy most prominently with his family. An Army colonel with two tours in Iraq, he wound up in the men's therapy group after his wife kicked him out of the house, tired of his control tactics and abuse. Though he'd never been a man's man or tough guy, he believed he should be the commander in every aspect of his life.

When Gerald finally opened up after ten months in the group, he admitted he'd been fearful that emotionality was "dangerously contagious." Three years later, having found an intimacy in relationships he'd never before experienced, Gerald viewed emotional candor as a badge of courage. One day, he told the group that Jane wouldn't take him back. "It was just too late. Too much water over the dam." Over the next couple years, Gerald grieved his loss. During one session, Mark, another group member, paused, looked at him and said, "Gerald, sometime you'll meet another woman."

"Yeah," Gerald replied, "But next time, I don't want to be a commander."

"You don't seem like much of a tyrant anymore."

"I guess I'm a different kind of guy."

"Yup. You've learned how to do relationships."

It was too late for Gerald to save his marriage, but not to save the rest of his life.

* * * * * * *

In 1973, ten years after *The Feminine Mystique* was published, Friedan wrote the following as a reflection on the era when the book first came out:

How could women and men ever really know or love each other as long as we kept playing those roles that kept us from knowing or being ourselves? Weren't men as well as women still locked up in lonely isolation, alienation, no matter how many sexual acrobatics we put their bodies through? Weren't men dying too young, suppressing fears and tears and their own tenderness? It seemed to me that men weren't really the enemy – they were fellow victims, suffering an outmoded masculine mystique that made them feel unnecessarily inadequate when there were no bears to kill.

Forty years later, many men have made scant progress while women have taken significant strides. It's hard to remember that not long ago the only jobs for women were nurse or teacher, and they couldn't open a bank account or buy a house without a man's co-signature. Certainly much work remains to be done before full equality is achieved, but many women are free of their mother's roles, while men seem stuck in the footsteps of their fathers. Men live an outmoded masculinity that's unfit for an information economy and unattractive to women who want a partner rather than a husband.

3

The Promise of Change

Many people are skeptical about men's capacity for change, and men's frequent initial resistance to engaging in work toward personal growth underscores this skepticism. They are particularly fearful of group therapy treatment and sometimes delay their first session. Ivan promised he'd come for his first group session but didn't show up until a month later. He later admitted that the three previous Tuesdays he'd driven to the group, parked, walked to the door of the building, and retreated to the car just before entering. Ivan was like the cop who admitted he'd had the courage to chase down an armed criminal, but sitting in a room with a group of other guys and talking about personal stuff scared the hell out of him.

Even when they do attend group treatment, men often try to protect themselves from participating. When they're newly court-mandated they'll boisterously proclaim, "This is a bunch of crap, and you guys may need to be here, but I sure as hell don't." Or, new to a therapy group, they may say the right things – "I can see I'm going to learn a lot here" – but their lack of authenticity is apparent to everyone.

When we started doing this work in the early 1990s, men's fear of therapy was seen as a real obstacle to treatment. The prevalent belief in psychological circles was this: since the values of socialized masculinity were antithetical to a milieu of effective therapy, men's progress would be arduous if not impossible. Ronald Levant, author of *Masculinity Reconstructed: Changing the Rules of Manhood – At Work, in Relationships and in Family Life,* coined the term "normative male alexithymia" to describe men's greater problems with expressing their emotions, and subsequent aversion to treatment.

Given the power of the man-pact and influence of the man-pack, the transition to what we call a "liberated male" is a hard sell. It takes strength and courage for men to move into self-exploration and transformation. They are being asked to question and defy what they have been taught throughout their lives. In the process they will most likely feel emasculated and risk marginalization from other members of the pack. Some may not see the prize at the end – emotional literacy and relational health – as worth the struggle. As recently as 2010, Gary Brooks, in *Beyond the Crisis of Masculinity,* asserted:

> Conventional psychotherapy [works] best when the client is able to self-disclose, relinquish control, recognize and express feelings, experience vulnerability, introspect, confront pain and relationship conflict, admit failure or ignorance, and manage nonsexual intimacy.

> Unfortunately, traditional masculine socialization teaches men to hide private experiences, exert maintain control, maintain stoicism, present the self as invincible, favor action over introspection, avoid relationship conflict, and sexualize intimate relationships. With this in mind, we can see how difficult it would be to create an environment that could possibly be any more uncomfortable for men's most preferred ways of being.

Better than Expected

In fact, over the years, generalized client resistance and gender-specific male qualities of suspicion, emotionlessness, and invulnerability have turned out to be far less damaging when men are treated in a men's therapy group. Certainly it's true that for many men the discomfort of their first group session is almost overwhelming. Not only are they in a small room with six or eight guys they've never met, but they are also hearing these men say things they couldn't imagine a man admitting. For example, in a session where the topic turns to shame, an elder – a guy who's been in the group for awhile – reveals that at one time he lost a job after getting caught by his colleague while masturbating to porn at work. Another guy relates that he used to get so drunk there were times he blacked out driving home with his young children in the back seat.

But men's therapy groups that start out as unnerving environments quickly become safe places when new members, eager to belong, find themselves following the model of other guys and making remarkable disclosures of their own.

Since the strongest force in men's lives is probably the need to belong to the "man-pack," therapists who run men's groups harness this ancient energy to create a camaraderie that helps them explore the brave new world of self-disclosure, emotionality, and intimacy. It's the power of a new pack that invites men down the path to resocialization and recovery.

Beyond exploring the symptoms of their male clients in different terms, men-centered therapists reverse some orthodox methodologies and find other remarkably effective treatment techniques. These include:

Stepping aside. In traditional groups, the therapist runs the show. In men's group sessions, therapists know when to step aside as elders model self-disclosure for new clients. Men's eyes are opened when they realize that the rules of men's therapy conduct diverge from all their previous experiences. Many who come to men's therapy groups have seldom, if ever, disclosed the dark side of their lives. So it's astounding to realize that it's safe to tell some of their deepest secrets to not just one man, but a group of men. They find that not only will they not suffer ridicule or rejection for speaking of their hidden humiliations, they are welcomed into the group. For most men, self-disclosure in men's groups opens up a new world of relationship; conversations previously limited to sports and cars grow to foster an intimacy they couldn't have imagined.

Modeling self-disclosure. Many therapists who work with men break the rule they learned in "Counseling 101" – never talk about themselves to clients. Instead, these therapists role model open self-talk, encouraging group members to reveal themselves. In the process, group leaders decrease hierarchy and model equality.

Reframing masculine values. Writing in *Voice Male*, a leading magazine on men and men's issues, Michael Kimmel, sociologist and author of numerous books on men and masculinity, sums up a new gestalt of manhood that clients learn in men's groups.

> We need men who truly embody traditional masculine virtues, such as strength, a sense of purpose…self-reliance, dependability, reliability, responsibility – men for whom these are not simply fashion accessories but come from a deeply interior place. But now these will be configured in new and responsive ways.

> We need men who are secure enough in their convictions to recognize a mistake, courageous enough to be compassionate, fiercely egalitarian, powerful enough to empower others, strong enough to acknowledge that real strength comes from holding others up rather than pushing them down and that real freedom is not to be found in the loneliness of the log cabin but in the daily compromises of life in a community.

The alternate universe of the group. The men's group creates a vision and experience of what life without mascupathy could look like. Instead of verbal jousting, men speak of their real concerns, really listening to and affirming one another. They begin living out the reconfiguration of masculine values as Kimmel envisions. They learn that vulnerability is not an act of weakness but of courage. Beyond that, effective treatment for men avoids a "scared straight" approach, but also demands accountability. It rests on a process of engagement in the group, something that could take many years for some individuals, but which stays with men for the rest of their lives. Here's the life-changing insight of Frank, who'd been in the group for four years when he summarized his experience.

> *I thought I was the coolest guy ever if I could hook up with one woman in the morning and another at night. They weren't relationships; women were just, you know, attracted to me. But when I look back, I almost always felt crappy afterward – I was ashamed – because it's not what I believe is morally right. Some of these women were in love with me, and I was just screwing them.*

Then I got involved with Marcia and tried to stop screwing other women. I'd gotten into this group, and knew I didn't want to cheat on Marcia, but one day I was walking home from work, and there was Helen with whom I'd flirted forever. We went up to her place. Afterwards, she said let's get together again, and I said I couldn't because by then I was living with Marcia.

Helen got pissed off and a couple days later called Marcia and told her what had happened, adding that I'd also been with lots of other women. Marcia was really hurt and angry. She wouldn't see me or talk to me for a few weeks. I really felt bad about hurting her. But in the long run it turned out to be a good thing. Our long talks – about what I did and how it affected her and if we'd stay together and how I'd keep on going to counseling – that was the first actual intimate emotional experience in my life with another person that wasn't sexual. It made me realize not only just how much I hurt her, but how much I loved her. It opened up a whole new world of relationship for me.

It's been three years now since we got together, and two years since I cheated on her, and I feel like I've been reborn. I have to tell you that without the group, I don't think it would have ever happened. She believed in me and you guys in the group believed in me. Her trust in me was the most important thing, but it wouldn't have happened without James and Vern and Robert and Mick. You guys taught me what closeness and support are really like.

An Awakening

The beginning of patriarchy's end is upon us, though not without considerable pushback from those who champion men as inherently dominant and immune to change. *ScienceDaily*, a web-based magazine that provides accounts of scientific research, reports that studies at University of California, Berkeley are challenging long-held beliefs that human beings are wired for the "survival of the fittest." In fact, researchers are finding evidence to show human beings – including men – are evolving to become more compassionate and collaborative in their quest to survive and thrive.

Dacher Keltner, a UC Berkeley psychologist and author of *Born to be Good: The Science of a Meaningful Life*, has concluded that the human capacity to care and cooperate is wired into particular regions of the brain and nervous system. One study found that people with a particular variation of the oxytocin gene receptor are more adept at reading the emotional state of others, and therefore are less stressed under tense circumstances. Informally known as the "cuddle hormone," oxytocin is secreted into the bloodstream and the brain, where it promotes social interaction, nurturing, and romantic love among other functions.

The *ScienceDaily* report concludes, "In contrast to 'every man for himself' interpretations of Charles Darwin's theory of evolution by natural selection, Keltner and his fellow social scientists are building the case that humans are successful as a species precisely because of our nurturing, altruistic, and compassionate traits. They call it 'survival of the kindest.'"

A kinder and newly fit man is definitely emerging. Like consumers trading in their flip-phones for smart phones, many men are now rejecting the four old rules of manhood that social scientists Deborah David and Robert Brannon identified in 1976: "No sissy stuff, be a big wheel, be a sturdy oak, and give 'em hell." They are, instead, finding that the "fittest" male is no longer the most aggressive or autonomous, but the man who is willing to work on himself, be introspective and relational. "Liberated men," often impacted by treatment, are becoming the provocateurs in wider, positive change in masculine ideology.

PART II

Origins of Tough Guys and Disappointing Partners

4

The Assault on Boys

Boys are born for intimacy. They love to climb into their dads' laps and cling to their moms' legs. They tussle affectionately with their siblings and other boys. They are made for sensitivity. They cry when they forget the travel monkey on a trip and are told they can't go back to get him, or when they wake up from a scary dream. When they're young, boys are uninhibited in their intimacy – rubbing Mom's silk scarf between their thumb and index finger or talking softly with Grandpa while they snuggle and nap after Sunday dinner.

By the time they're four or five, at untold expense to themselves and, years later, to women and their own children, boys have been kicked off their dads' laps and taught to fight rather than play. Their ability to empathize, which according to research conducted by Martin Hoffmann, author of *Sex Differences in Empathy and Related Behaviors*, is equal to girls' in infancy, has been socialized out of them. Their connective capacity – much of their marvelous openness, affection, and excitement – has been relentlessly cut away from them through repeated, painful experience.

The invasive procedure of male socialization transforms easy-going and fun-loving boys into tough guys and distant partners. It is an assault that skews a more balanced inherent masculinity and severely restricts men's range of emotionality and intimacy. The psychological history of every man is a chronicle of his losing struggle with socialization. This is the story Randy shared while modeling self-disclosure with his men's therapy group:

It's a sunny and cold Saturday morning in Northern Michigan. Our beagle, Queenie, taps her nails rhythmically on the tiled kitchen floor. My father takes his 12-gauge shotgun from the cabinet. I nervously lace my snow boots up, trying to hurry so that I don't hold up Dad and my two older brothers.

This is my first hunt. For years I've watched them go off without me. I'm proud and excited as I watch my brothers follow Dad's command to head to the top of a brush pile, a favorite place of refuge for a rabbit on the run.

We come to the edge of a swamp, and Queenie starts barking like mad. Dad looks back at me and holds his palm out signaling me to stop and be quiet. Suddenly, we see a rabbit running along the edge of the swamp ahead of Queenie, heading for the brush pile. My heart begins pounding as Dad pulls up the gun, takes aim, and boom! He misses. Just as quickly, something changes inside me, and I start to shake as I watch the empty shell tumble into the snow. Pump, and boom again! I look up and this time I see the impact of the shot throwing the rabbit up into the air. Then it's on the ground, rolling over, tiny feet pawing at the frozen earth.

I look away and then back. The rabbit's flailing has turned to twitches, blood coursing out of its little body, matting its brown and white fur a bright red. Dad grasps the dying rabbit's back legs in his strong hands and holds the rabbit upside down. I'm mesmerized. What is he going to do next? With one karate chop to the back of the head; he kills the rabbit. At least it's dead now, I think, and then – I can't believe it – my father twists the rabbit's head off and throws it into the brush. I stand frozen while Queenie excitedly licks the blood from the beheaded rabbit. I blink back tears as my lips begin to tremble.

Dad is dressing the rabbit, and I hope he's too preoccupied to notice me. He isn't. Spinning around, he sees me crying. "What the heck is wrong with you?" he barks.

Several years later, my little sister goes hunting with us. By now I have learned to act like a man. Like me on my first hunt,

58

Debbie bursts out crying at the brutality. But it's different with her. Derisive and harsh when I cried, Dad soothes Debbie, comforts her. She doesn't need to learn to "suck it up." She never goes hunting again.

Randy was elated at the prospect of hunting that day – finding a new camaraderie with his big brothers and dad. Without knowing the words, he understood this was an initiation, that it could be the first true act of manhood. Though his struggle to stretch his short legs into the footsteps of his dad's long gait was perhaps a sign he was not ready, he was completely unprepared for the brutality of hunting.

Randy's story isn't about the ethics of killing animals; it's about learning to shut down feelings and "act like a man." It was a lesson for him, and virtually every other boy, handed down by his father from the ancient wisdom of the man-pact, one of the many principles that are repeated until it impacts his every behavior. Like every kid, Randy wanted his father's approval. He tried to keep his horror hidden and, failing, evoked his dad's ridicule. Over the next few years he built an armor of invulnerability around himself, not only for desensitizing himself to the blood of the hunt, but also for every aspect of the psychic brutality of being a man.

Thinking back on it, Randy realizes a big piece of his heart froze as hard as the Michigan ground that day. He shut down. Back at the house, Randy's brother said, "Great hunt, huh?" At that moment, Randy learned to lie about what went on in his belly. "Yup," he said, "very cool." Randy went underground, especially with his feelings. It would be years before he coaxed them to the surface, and felt them beginning to thaw.

Judy Chu, research scientist and lecturer at Stanford University, explains that, like Randy, most boys learn what is considered appropriate and desirable behavior and also the consequences of deviating from accepted norms. She suggests that as boys adapt to society and culture, they move from "presence to pretense via posturing." They:

- Learn to anticipate how others will respond to them and accordingly modify their self-expression and styles of relating to others

- Become more selective and strategic about what they reveal and to whom
- Begin to shield their thoughtful self-reflection, deep interpersonal understanding, and relational capabilities in order to protect their vulnerability.

Just as they reach the age where emotional intimacy with parents and friends could be most beneficial, boys learn to disconnect from themselves and others. The security of grade school is replaced by the peer pressure of middle school. The need for emotional closeness and self-awareness is hijacked by the desire to "fit in."

Constructs, not reality. A boy's self-concept, his growing sense of himself as a boy and a man, is not primarily a product of *inherent* masculine qualities in his psyche. Certainly there are some genetic aspects of men – their physical size and muscularity incline them to take the role of protector and aggressor – but primarily, manhood is defined by socialization. As we continued to grow in our work with boys and men, we became even more convinced that stereotyped depictions and cartoon-like characterizations exaggerate dissimilarities between genders, exacerbating distance between men and women. In fact, boys are genetically engineered with both masculine and feminine traits.

Masculinity and femininity, like other descriptors of personality, are constructs, not reality. While men and women surely have inherent anatomical differences, these are not innate and durable masculine or feminine organic structures, which rigidly control the gender roles of the human psyche. Masculinity and femininity are amorphous, changing, adaptive.

You hear people say, *you can never understand a man – or a woman* – and John Gray offered new and helpful perspectives when he pointed out telling differences. Women often do have greater need to tell their stories, and men more desire to hole up in their caves. But Gray's popular book's catchy title, *Men are from Mars, Women Are from Venus,* overemphasizes differences and magnifies an unfortunate misconception.

In his book, *The Gendered Society*, Kimmel suggests that, "many of the differences between women and men that we observe in our everyday lives are actually not gender differences at all, but differences that are the result of being in different positions or in different arenas. The positions themselves elicit the behaviors we see as gendered. Differences among women and men are far greater than the mean differences between women and men." Bottom line: men possess more qualities referred to as "masculine" than those termed "feminine." More, not *only*.

Human ancestry. Anthropologists such as Michael Ghiglieri, author of *The Dark Side of Man: Tracing the Origins of Male Violence*, have maintained that human ancestors were chimpanzees who exemplified hierarchal civilizations and used violence as the primary way to resolve conflict.

Some recent research in primate psychology has, however, begun to transform our understanding of men and their behavior. Primatologist Frans B. M. de Waal, professor of Primate Behavior at Emory University, suggested a different view when he published his studies of another primate, bonobos, noting that they too are human ancestors but they represent an egalitarian and conciliatory way of life. His research suggests that men, at heart, are much more diverse than binary socialization has made them.

Taken together, chimps and bonobos – both human cousins and forebears – provide a rounded and more accurate view of the innate male psyche. Chimps demonstrate aggression and self-interest; bonobos epitomize mutuality, a society in which conflict is, amazingly enough, settled with lovemaking.

De Waal compares the human brain "to a Swiss army knife to which evolution has added models for everything from face recognition and tool use to child care and friendship." Unfortunately, for too many men the wonder of their childhood and the vulnerability of intimate friendship have been subsumed by socialization that maintains the conventional view of male psyches and behavior. If men find their second bonobo nature, we believe they will achieve a balance, leading to negotiation rather than hostility, affinity instead of distance, and empathy over derision.

The second voice. As different as they may appear, there is a connection between the emotional distancing of a relationally-deficient male partner and the lethal acts of men such as the Newtown, Connecticut mass murderer. Both possess an *only choice*

61

mindset that typifies the insular and aggressive behavior of the chimp while rejecting *the second voice* of the bonobo: conciliation. Although recent human history, including events of the early twenty-first century, has borne the bad news that aggressive primate ancestry is the dominant force behind most men's behavior, it is at least clear that some men now listen to the second voice.

5

Hidden Feelings that Deaden Men's Souls

Society needs law enforcement to keep it safe, and our country needs a strong military to protect our shores. Our streets harbor criminals, and we have both foreign and domestic enemies. Clearly there have been and will be many times when we must defend ourselves. We require tough, aggressive men and women who possess the will and capacity to assault and kill. But aggression gets a bad name because men, in particular, are sometimes more aggressive than necessary, leading to a focus on men's aggressiveness that distracts us from the real problem and its solution.

The common description of men as aggressive, competitive, and egotistical emphasizes the *behavior* rather than the troika of *emotional causes*: fear, shame, and loneliness. Because men are not allowed to show emotion, it's hard to imagine that their psyches are driven by feelings which the man-pack exploits as motivators of behavior. But men's conscious and unconscious lives are dominated by *fear* of reprisal from other men for inadequate manliness and avoidance of *shame* for unmanly softness and frailty. Worse, the pain of these core emotions is exacerbated by loneliness. Many other qualities – lust, hurt, sadness, hope, love – play a part in men's psyches, but none come close to the impact of fear, shame, or loneliness.

The Emotional Foundation of Men's Difficult Lives

Charlie recalls. *I'm in seventh grade, kind of a nerdy kid. We carpool to Boy Scouts every week; five of us learning how to build things out of wood and make campfires. My mother drives. I sit in the backseat in the middle, and out of nowhere, Jimmy hits me hard in the side knocking the wind out of me. It really hurts, and I can't help but let out a small cry as I gasp for air. I literally try to suck it up because I don't want my mother to know what's happened. The next week and the weeks thereafter, I try not to sit in the back with Jimmy, yet somehow I end up there and he hits me again and again. After a while, I quit Boy Scouts.*

In retrospect, Charlie realizes that by the time he was thirteen, he had already learned some core rules of the man-pact: hide pain and never let a woman, even your mother, see you've been attacked without fighting back. Smaller and weaker than most boys, Charlie was afraid to hit Jimmy back; he knew yelling "Stop that!" would be the equivalent of "telling on" him, violating the man-pact. The other boys could do worse than knock the wind out of him. Hiding physical pain, concealing embarrassment, Charlie saw himself as an inadequate male. So young, and already so much shame.

Charlie was sure his mom heard his muffled cry each time Jimmy hit him; that she listened for it, fearful she'd hear it again, which of course she did. But just as Charlie didn't know what to do, she didn't know how to handle the situation either. Still, she probably knew enough about the male code to purposefully make the decision not to protect him – not to endanger his fragile manhood – and so she, too, did nothing.

When they got home, Charlie could have said, "Jimmy keeps hitting me. What should I do?" But he already was ashamed. He feared his mom would shame him more, asking, "Charlie, what's the matter with you that you don't stand up for yourself?" She might even tell his father. So neither of them mentioned what happened on the way. Instead, they colluded in silence. For Charlie, silence was worse than Jimmy knocking the wind out of him. Even more painful was the psychic pain that his failure to live up to the man-pact was so shameful it couldn't be mentioned, especially to who was then the most important woman in his life.

The Troika of Dark Emotions

Dark emotion #1: Fear. Charlie was not a poor student of the man-pact. He knew full-well the code of conduct, and he'd countless times heard its reinforcement by the man-pack. But he feared the outcome of attacking back on those trips to Boy Scouts. The ache in his abdomen told him he wasn't manly enough, so he found an emotional corner away from everybody else and just shut down. He knew you don't tell anybody the dirty secret of inadequate masculinity. Sick as it made him, he had realized he just had to live with it.

Like Charlie, most boys are excellent students in their crash course in acceptable male behavior. Early on, they learn to fear from searing reprimands that come early and often from their fathers, coaches, and other boys: *Don't cry like a girl. Fight back. Stop acting like a sissy. Don't let anybody get in your way.* Well before kindergarten, *many* boys have been instructed: *Act like a man!*

They quickly learn the right names to call boys who don't live up to the pact. *Mama's boy. Girl. Sissy! Bitch! Pussy! Faggot!* What's mostly not recognized is that name-calling is not mere taunting; it's a barrage of teaching moments. Beyond admonishments from their fathers *and mothers,* boys soon realize that other boys will push them around and take their toys. While appearing to experience the simple joy of chasing each other around in the backyard, they have already adopted a wary vigilance: five-year-olds watching out for the six-year-old bully. Even that young, they know there are often bigger boys waiting to chase them down.

Beyond the verbal attack, chances are pretty good that boys have been hit by a parent or another boy. Deep in their psyches, they apprehend that other boys and men are dangerous, that males who don't conform to the strict and restrictive standards of the man-pact are vulnerable not just to verbal abuse, but also to physical abuse and assault.

Early lessons. There are other major aspects of boys' early training. First, the man-pack has chosen its words carefully so they'll have a dual impact. The names that boys get called are virtually always feminine – sissy, bitch, girl, pussy – and boys learn not only to avoid feminine behavior, they also incorporate the mascupathic principle that the feminine is inferior, to be disrespected and ridiculed. In his book, *Half-Lived Life*, John Lee states that, "The rejection of all things associated with 'the feminine' is one of men's greatest regressions." Long before they know the word "misogyny," boys learn that girls are to be denigrated and women seen as chattel and objects of pleasure.

Second, in addition to learning that disrespect for and objectification of women are to be valued, boys learn that homosexuality gets men ridiculed, beaten, and sometimes murdered, and any thought or behavior that has even the scent of "gay" is to be castigated and renounced. They learn to believe that there is nothing worse than being gay. It's not surprising that many gay men hid in the proverbial closet before deciding persecution was more tolerable than inauthenticity.

Third, boys are taught one "approved" emotion: anger. Since they've learned the outcomes of showing fear or shame, they unconsciously begin to incorporate the life-long tactic of turning dark feelings into anger, numbing the panic of fear and the nausea of shame with manly aggression. Here's how one man instinctively morphed his fright into rage.

Simon hadn't paid much attention to his wife, Maureen, for a long time; he was always busy with something. One evening, she told him that she was thinking about leaving him: she wanted to make a life of her own. Simon was blindsided and stupefied with fear: he had never thought of a life without Maureen. But his panic came out as loud belligerence, and he screamed at her that she was so incompetent she could never make it without him. It was a behavior that, of course, only drove her further away and she moved out the next week.

Strains of fear. Anxiety is generalized fear, often brought about by frequent stress. In *The Myth of Masculinity*, Joseph Pleck opened a new window when he portrayed men's anxiety about being male as "gender role strain." He described three pervasive fears resulting from the experience of attempting to live within conventional male roles:

- **Trauma Strain.** The anxiety of repeated trauma from boyhood male socialization and its reinforcement during adulthood.

- **Discrepancy Strain.** The trepidation of the inability to meet traditional male gender role standards set so high that no man ever completely meets them.
- **Dysfunction Strain.** The angst when fulfillment of male gender roles through externalization behaviors such as substance abuse, affairs, or hyper-competitiveness runs counter to moral beliefs.

Living with these stresses, most men respond to life events with inappropriate reactivity. On the one hand, they come to perceive trifling matters as traumatic; for instance, the woman driving in front of them in the left turn lane who stops for the yellow light. On the other hand, they grow immune to the assaults of life resulting in a state of continual hyper-arousal and often show virtually no emotional response to traumatic news, like a loved one getting cancer. They have instead developed a series of cognitions that the world is harsh, a place where they'll be victims of others' bad intentions if they aren't vigilant.

Fear expressed as vigilance. Candice Batton, director of the School of Criminology and Criminal Justice at the University of Nebraska, Omaha points out, "The majority of all homicide perpetrators are male – approximately 90-91 percent.... Males may be more likely to be violent, especially lethally violent, than females because they are more likely than females to develop negative attributions of blame that are external in nature, that is: 'The cause ... of my problems is someone else or some force outside of me.' And this translates into anger and hostility toward others as well as wary vigilance and angry over-reactivity."

Our clinical observations suggest that men's pattern of generalized vigilance is a deep and abiding form of stress, and can be termed Post-Traumatic Stress Syndrome (PTSS). Although many men appear confident and powerful, their fears and anxieties, stresses and strains, leave them guarded and fragile beneath their armor. In group therapy, men spill out the stress and trauma of bullying, ridicule, and rejection – both psychic and physical injuries – that they've concealed from others and from themselves. PTSS doesn't produce the most striking dysfunctions, such as the devastating flashbacks of its cousin, Post-Traumatic Stress Disorder (PTSD), but it so consistently consumes men that it creates an internal structure of anxiety and agitation that often quashes their attempts at compassion and concern for others.

Don had never experienced the trauma of war or watched his child die after a car accident, but his life had been traumatic nonetheless. Although he owned a highly successful computer design firm, his inner life was unsettling. He told the men's therapy group about his critical father who repeatedly focused on what Don had done wrong rather than right. When Don was seven years old and sweeping the garage, his father would point out the places Don had missed, angrily berating his insufficient work, and then make him start over.

Don also revealed that his scrawniness left him victim to bigger boys and he took the long way home from school to avoid bullies. His first wife cheated on him, which led to drunken debaucheries that left him feeling disgusted with himself. Nevertheless, he quickly turned into a full-blown alcoholic.

He told the group of his numerous failed attempts to stop drinking. Not only did the world seem a minefield of potential disasters, but, far worse, after repeated relapses he'd concluded that he couldn't trust himself, that he was actually a greater threat to himself than any other entity in his life.

In his four years of therapy, Don realized that fear was the cause of many of his problems including bellicosity towards his bosses, eschewal of serious relationships, and diversion into gambling and pornography. He finally achieved long-term sobriety, but though his powers of self-observation had grown, self-governance was still not fully-realized. It would be another five years before he learned to manage his fears and find fulfilling relationships.

Dark emotion #2: Shame. Of the dark emotions, shame is the most devastating. Hurt drives men into caves of isolation, denudes relationships, and fear strips them of the capacity to risk opening their hearts. But shame destroys the soul. It has been called *the loathing feeling* which is directed more at self than others and breeds life-stealing self-contempt.

There are of course forms of shame that are natural and healthy. Embarrassment reminds people of their humanity: A man's mild shame at forgetting to zip up his fly is a nostalgic remembrance of his father's gentle reminders of what to do before he comes out of the bathroom. Shame can also serve as a helpful admonition: A young man has just got his learner's permit, and after a near accident his father warns him, "You've got to watch your side-view mirrors when you're driving."

The nauseating state of feeling that therapist and educator John Bradshaw explains as toxic in *Healing the Shame that Binds You* is certainly neither wistful nor constructive. It robs people of healthy self-regard. Psychoanalyst, Helen B. Lewis was a pioneer when, in 1971, she pointed out in *Shame and Guilt in Neurosis*, "The experience of shame is directly about the self, which is the focus of evaluation. In guilt, the self is not the central object of negative evaluation, but rather the thing done is the focus." Put another way, guilt is: *I did something wrong.* Shame is: *I am wrong.* Kirk Brink, psychologist on the faculty of the Institute for Individual and Group Therapy, adds this telling point. "It really isn't fear *and* shame; it's fear *of* shame."

Toxic shame often has disastrous consequences. In *Violence: Reflections on a National Epidemic*, James Gilligan M.D., Harvard Professor and Director of Mental Health for the Massachusetts Prison System, concludes, "If the solid undifferentiated black nuclei in cells under the microscope are markers for carcinoma, so shame is the marker in a psychological test report for the presence of the potential for violence." Men who choose violence do so in order to regain empowerment, keep their distance in relationships out of fear of further shame, and act out in substance abuse and sex to dampen down feelings of indignity. What they don't realize is that aggression, avoidance, and externalization only intensify shame.

> *Like so many other men, Duncan escaped into two-hour workouts to ward off the shame that he got fired from his job for stealing tools from the shop. Then, shamed because his wife had become the breadwinner, he reverted to machismo to prove his manhood and got into a fight over who was first in line for a movie. When the police came and told him to leave the scene, he endured even more shame as he and his wife returned home to sit in silence, watching TV re-runs.*

In his most recent book, *Angry White Men: Masculinity at the End of An Era*, Kimmel introduced a new dynamic of shame called "aggrieved entitlement." Because men hold a hierarchical view of the world, some (especially white, heterosexual men) claim supremacy over other men and women, believing that they, not those they consider inferior, have certain rights. For example, they often think they are entitled to the promotion at work or to make the decisions at home. Such men become indignant, resentful, and most of all, shamed when they perceive that other people have seized their power and influence in the workplace and neighborhoods as well as in institutions such as marriage.

Sometimes these shame-filled men act out their grievances in verbal rage toward the person who has affronted them; other times, like Duncan, they vent their humiliation in arbitrary assault. Still other men grieve their stolen entitlements by withdrawing into a malaise of cynical and apathetic depression. Failing to accept the rightness of egalitarianism, to cross-train themselves for a new world of work and equal partnerships at home, they simply shut themselves down – victims whose main escape is griping to other men at the bar about the unfairness of it all.

Shame reinforced. The shame that's learned in childhood from critical parents and traumatic events is reinforced with daily adult bullying. Beyond recurrent painful experience, the mind's tendency to compare and contrast current events to past experiences casts a dark shadow over the present.

> *Harry met Lawrence walking down the hall at work. Usually friendly, Lawrence didn't respond when Harry said a friendly hello. Harry's well-intended but errant unconscious mind brought up comparable shaming events: as a kid, his grandfather (who had grown deaf) didn't respond to him; his dad didn't return his call for two weeks (he was out of the country); his wife was sexually unresponsive (she was abused as a child).*

> *These disturbing touchstones cast a long shadow over the present trivial event, and Harry quickly lost his psychic balance, finding himself asking the same lightning questions: What did I do to Lawrence? How come nobody pays attention to me? Why do I always piss other people off? And a conclusion: People start out liking me, and then I screw things up. God, I hate myself.*

Harry's unconscious mind dipped into the vat of the body's shaming biopharmaceuticals – among them cortisol, the stress hormone – and produced raging feelings of self-recrimination and humiliation. The reality was that Lawrence's unresponsiveness had nothing to do with Harry; Lawrence was incommunicative because he was enduring his own shame, having just come from the boss' office where he'd been put on probation.

If men didn't live in fear of shame for asking the wrong questions, Harry might have questioned Lawrence about his lack of response and learned its actual cause. Instead, Harry entered a labyrinth of searing memories, self-recriminations, and fallacious conclusions.

Shame of self-disclosure. At some point in their lives, most males take the risk of revealing themselves to another boy or man, usually disclosing something sexual.

Quentin had done something he was ashamed of and he had heard on a talk show that talking about it will clear the mind. So he told an old college buddy, who was also his best friend, that he cheated on his wife one time and that it was with her sister. Quentin expected his friend, Robert, to laugh it off, but that didn't happen. Instead, Robert says, "What the hell is wrong with you? Wow, that's terrible. You're despicable."

Robert's response set off a series of larger humiliations for Quentin: the shame of making the mistake of revealing his horrible secret, surpassed by the shame Quentin feels every time he runs into Robert at the gym, and ultimately, generating the fear of further shame that Robert will tell every guy who belongs to the health club about Quentin's indiscretion. The event and the cascade of fears drove Quentin to adopt a principle that voids relationship: "I'll never tell anybody another damn thing about my life."

The greatest fear. Fear *and* shame are the dark feelings, but it was Quentin's fear *of* shame that drove him to shut down his life. Paul Gilbert, author of *Shame: Interpersonal Behavior, Psychopathology, and Culture*, points out that men with shame are "people for whom life is a battle, who feel they have to earn their love and defend their place in the world." It's a hard life when you always come from a defensive posture.

Brene Brown, who presents research with humor and frank, personal discernments, summarizes the malevolent emotion in her book *Daring Greatly: How the Courage to be Vulnerable Transforms the Way We Live, Love, Parent and Lead.* "Shame is universal," she says, "but the messages and expectations that drive shame are organized by gender.... Men... need to stop feeling, start earning, put everyone in their place, and climb their way to the top or die trying. Push open the lid of your box to grab a breath of air, or slide that curtain back a bit to see what's going on, and BAM! shame cuts you down to size."

Manifestations of shame. Glen Gabbard, Professor of Clinical Psychiatry at Baylor University, cites two different manifestations of shame in men. First, the *oblivious* type – grandiose, arrogant, and seemingly thick-skinned – for whom it's hard to imagine that shame is the trigger. Second, the *hyper-vigilant* type – easily hurt, over-sensitive, neurotic – whose pathetic presentation makes shame obvious and for whom sympathy is a challenge.

The oblivious man demands admiration, envy, and appreciation, pushing people away; the hyper-vigilant male neutralizes his self-devaluation by seeing others as unjust abusers and playing the victim, a particularly unattractive life-role.

Men seldom express shame in a way that induces understanding and empathy. Both oblivious and hyper-vigilant men break out in shame attacks that they erroneously view as panic attacks. Unfortunately, their partners often experience these attacks as unprovoked and misdirected rage. Whether men close their arms tightly across their chests to hold shame in, or express it in an angry outburst that shakes the dishes in the china cabinet, shame pushes people away, leading to the third dark force: loneliness.

This is the dark paradoxical problem with shame: Its message is that you need to hide and keep shameful secrets or you'll create more shame, when, in fact, acknowledging shameful events in the right place with the right people is what heals and dissipates shame.

Dark emotion #3: Loneliness. The pain of loneliness is more than a lack of guys to pal around with or people with whom to share successes and hurts. The need to bond with others is hard-wired into human beings – especially in men who are out there on the rough terrain of a seemingly savage world – and when there are no bonds with other men, it's easy to become anxious. Unlike their male ancestors for whom the group was necessary for survival, most of today's American men don't face greater life-threats if they don't belong to a protective group, but the angst of not belonging is still there.

In *A Slender Thread*, Diane Ackerman explains the genetic fear that loneliness creates. When people lived in caves, she says, and faced "hunger, the elements, territory disputes, and wild animals, belonging to a loyal family group [was their] only hope. An aching need to belong becomes an instinct indisputable as rock. Not belonging is one of those things to dread and worry endlessly about." That ancient fear of not having safe, strong ties with other human beings still runs through men's psyches, but often male socialization won't allow men to reach out to one another in a way that would defray their anxiety.

Many men are detached, living in constant dread and endless worry, but they aren't able to look deep enough inside themselves to see that it's about loneliness. *Unrecognized, and therefore experienced as irritation, men view loneliness as inevitable.* Since they don't connect the dots, their seclusion begets more loneliness. And the real problem with loneliness is not only that it's a painful state in its own right, but that it serves as a catalyst – exacerbating fear and intensifying shame – by isolating the mind, leaving it vulnerable to even more distorted thinking.

> *Alone in his dark den, Walter watched his team win in overtime, and it occurred to him to call Duane and suggest they go to the next game together. But then he thought, "Why doesn't he ever call me?" bringing up feelings of rejection that turned loneliness into estrangement and alienation into rage. All in a matter of seconds, Walter decided, "The hell with it. I'll never call that jerk again in my life."*

Without the mind-clearing engagement with other people, telling him, "I know how that feels" or "Walter, that's a pretty normal reaction to things," his mind roams over the same self-contemptuous questions: Why don't I have any friends? How come nobody calls me? How come everybody else has a girlfriend? Why doesn't anybody like me?

Finally, shame in conjunction with loneliness is the great reason to drink, and alcoholism of course complicates everything. John Bradshaw disclosed his own experience of the lethal spiral in *Healing the Shame that Binds You*. "I used to drink," he wrote, "to solve the problems caused by drinking. The more I drank to relieve my shame-based loneliness and hurt, the more I felt ashamed."

Alcoholics Anonymous is effective because it presents the opportunity for the self-disclosure that heals shame and supplies unconditional acceptance from others, breaking the cycle and making a space for recovery.

Stunted Empathy

Larry called the therapy office to schedule an appointment because Carla told him she wanted a divorce. Not self-motivated for treatment, he was resistant and closed in his initial individual and group sessions. After a few months, the therapist asked him to invite Carla for several couple's sessions. They brought their three-year-old son, Christopher, with them.

Half-way through the session, Carla said, "It feels like I never do anything right. No matter what I do, he criticizes me." Larry's response boomed across the room. "That's bullshit. I don't criticize. That's crazy. You exaggerate everything."

Clearly startled and afraid, Carla turned away from him, stood up and walked across the office, kneeling down to work with Christopher on a puzzle. In disgust, Larry said, "See, she ignores me like that all the time. That's why I get so angry."

Later that week, Larry told the group about his couple counseling, expecting that the guys would see the incident like he did. In fact, they challenged him for not understanding how Carla felt. It could have been an important lesson in empathy, but Larry was too obsessed with vindicating himself to see it.

Some months later, Carla lost hope that Larry would ever change, and she moved on to make a new life. Larry left the group a couple weeks later, a man, at least for the foreseeable future, with a bleak life ahead, one that would probably include more harm to more women, children, and himself.

Empathy is an emotional connection to another person's experience. Two conditions contribute to cultivating empathy: affection and previous experience. Jerome, for example, experiences great empathy for his eight-year-old son who comes home crying after being bullied by older neighborhood kids. He loves his son, and he recalls what it was like to be bullied at that age.

The man-pack is contemptuous of empathy because it gets in the way. It can be an obstacle to meeting the requirements of the man-pact, and it can slow a man down in achieving masculine tasks.

Contemplate the quarterback's pain when you send him crashing to the ground, and you might miss the tackle. Ponder your co-worker's shame when you pick apart his new marketing plan, and you might lose your status as "champion" of the sales force. Empathy is not just a distraction; it can brand a man as a softie and a loser.

Empathy and morality are siblings. If a man's moral compass is inoperative, he loses his way, and his sense of masculinity can become so distorted that his psychic wiring short-circuits and he takes pleasure in another's pain: boys bully other boys to see them squirm. Some men don't grow up, and, as with Larry, they maim other people, sometimes emotionally, other times physically.

Social Toxicity

A small, anxious, and mildly cognitively impaired kid, Grant was regularly mocked, chased, and hit by older kids on the way to school. During the summer, desperate to avoid their bullying, he decided just to stay in the house. Then they started calling him on the phone. After several phone calls, Grant's mother complained to the boys' parents, who did nothing. They got an unlisted number, but the bullies continued to yell taunts at their house. Grant had officially been characterized as a "mama's boy."

When Grant graduated from high school, he became a recluse. But staying at home by himself took a toll, and, nervous, isolated, and angry, Grant's fear and frustration about his growing powerlessness reached a breaking point. One hazy, hot summer day, he stewed while watching television by himself. Looking out the window he noticed one of the bullies walking by on the street below. He felt a surge of rage. Before he knew what he was doing, he had his dad's handgun and ammunition. He opened the window and started shooting in the air. Nobody got hurt, but Grant was arrested. Although he had just turned 18, he was convicted of a felony: intentionally discharging a firearm at an occupied building. Grant's violent outburst put an indelible stain on his record; it changed the course of his life.

Some boys and men are clearly more susceptible to mascupathy than others. Why? According to James Garbarino, an expert on children and violence and the author of *Lost Boys: Why Our Sons Turn Violent and How We Can Save Them,* the cause is social toxicity, a concept Garbarino developed almost a quarter century ago. Just as physical toxins such as lead in the ground, carbon in the air, PCBs in the water, and pesticides in the food chain threaten the well-being of the most vulnerable humans, Garbarino asserts that social toxins such as violence, unemployment, poverty, disenfranchisement, and racism have similar impacts on human well-being. Just as the asthmatic individual is more affected by air pollution than others, certain vulnerable men are more affected by toxic male socialization and may become more mascupathic themselves.

Boys and men who live with such poisons, as well as those who have been oppressed by dominant power groups, grow raw to the touch. As risks accumulate, some attempt to reestablish their eroded sense of masculinity by acting particularly tough, amplifying an already distorted sense of their masculinity.

The experiences of many of the boys and men cited in these pages have been toxic, but they've found varying ways to cope. Randy's shutdown, Charlie's withdrawal, Simon's hostility, Jesse's avoidance, Walter's insularity, and Grant's impulsivity are desperate failed attempts to take charge of the bedlam of their psychic lives. On the very far end of the spectrum are shooters, those who end up shooting their way through their pain, exercising the ultimate act of control. Unable to manage their psychic agony – a tiny part of their larger psyches and physiology – these desperate males perceive ending life as their only choice.

PART III
New Directions

6

A Pathology of Masculinity

In the late nineteenth century, the medical profession developed the disease model to describe the physical causes, nature, and treatment of illness. This paradigm remains an essential assessment tool to determine if a particular phenomenon is a pathology.

Most people think of a disease as a dysfunction or failure in the structures of the mind or body. And there are certainly many mental health disorders that are a product of a chemical imbalance or physical health issues that are organic problems like cancer and heart disease. While that's one conception, a more accurate definition is this: *a medical construct that describes a group of observable causes and symptoms, codified and standardized over time.* For example, physiologically speaking there is no such thing as a cold. What is commonly called "a cold" is a group of symptoms that are caused by a virus. Calling this group of symptoms "a cold" is a convenience and, especially in the case of more serious diseases such as pneumonia, it provides diagnostic criteria and a regimen for treatment. Here is the rundown of the common cold which exhibits aspects of the disease model: *cause*, a virus; *symptoms*, runny nose, cough; *duration*, a week or two; *burdens*, fatigue, ache, sleep issues; *treatments*, rest and symptom reduction with aspirin and decongestants.

Mascupathy as disease. Our years spent observing and treating men confirmed our belief that the conventional disorders listed in the *DSM* didn't address the symptoms that we consistently observed in our male clients. We wanted a new understanding of masculinity that:

1. Defined the traits and issues of men as well as helped to develop and implement plans for psychoeducation, resocialization, and recovery
2. Provided, beyond the therapeutic world, a framework to see men more clearly, recognizing the commonality of their malaise and struggles
3. Asserted that men's behavior is not usually malicious or arbitrary, but a product of a socialization process that can create a psychological disorder
4. Recognized that men are *always* responsible for their behavior and to provide them tools to heal themselves and act with greater accountability.

Like other diseases, such as pneumonia, the severity of mascupathy and of its symptoms varies. As our anecdotal, clinical research indicates, mascupathy presents itself in five distinct types and subtypes which we cover in the next chapter. Here is how mascupathy, like the common cold, meets the criteria of a disorder using the disease model:

- Definable *cause:* to some degree genetics, but primarily male socialization
- Observable and relatively consistent *symptoms* ranging from grandiosity and self-aggrandizement to insularity and externalization
- Predictable *duration* of symptoms: lifelong, unless interrupted by resocializing treatment or a crisis, such as divorce, that motivates change
- Particular *burdens:* aggression, health problems, emotional inexpressiveness or reactivity, addiction, shortened lifespan, and difficulty in sustaining healthy long-term relationships
- *Treatment* of choice: long-term group experiential treatment with other men and engagement in a lifelong recovery program.

Mascupathy

Though it hasn't been clinically researched, our repeated observations consistently suggest that mascupathy is as real and pervasive as diagnoses listed in the *DSM* which includes arcane phobias of insects and frotteuristic disorder (touching and rubbing against a nonconsensual person). From our point of view, just because mascupathy is so common as to appear normal doesn't mean it's not a pathology.

Here are the three main components of mascupathy described in language typically used in psychiatric diagnoses:

1. Weak self-concept

A deficient or distorted sense of self, creating incongruence between thoughts/feelings and actions, resulting in withdrawal and insularity or impulsive and aggressive behavior:

- A pattern of inadequate or distorted sense of self, frequently resulting in personally and relationally damaging compensatory behaviors
- Difficulty in perceiving oneself clearly, and projection of self to others in exaggerated ways, i.e., arrogance and excessive confidence
- An unstable perception of self, leading to moodiness/fluctuating presentations of self
- Proclivity to lead a duplicitous life as evidenced by grandiosity, excessive fantasy, or a secret life of addictions or extramarital relationships to compensate for anxiety about one's self image
- The development of defensive belief systems, i.e., illusions of superiority, to compensate for feelings of fear and shame
- An excessive need to be admired to address feelings of inferiority (intimate partners chosen for their attractiveness, showy cars, ostentatious homes) and to buttress self-image before other men.

2. Inadequate emotionality

Persistent difficulty with experiencing, naming (alexithymia) managing, and expressing feelings which leads to shallow and conflictual relationships as well as pervasive impairment in the following two domains:

a. Emotional awareness

- Difficulty identifying and experiencing specific feelings (other than anger) resulting in inexplicable (to both self and other) hypersensitivity, social withdrawal, or vacillating moods, i.e., feelings of hurt that develop into irritability alternating with depression
- Inadequate capacity to discern the source of particular emotions resulting in misplaced emotions, i.e., disappointment in failure to receive a promotion at work leading to overreaction when a son fails to do chores
- Blunted emotionality as evidenced by fear of exhibiting joy or crying in situations when expressing such feelings would be appropriate
- Desensitization to acts of violence or cruelty that other people find disturbing
- Diminished sense of empathy, for example, difficulty in sharing the joy of another's success or sympathy for the loss of a loved one

b. Emotional management

- Externalization (acting out) to avoid painful feelings, including excessive use of substances, work, sex, or other activities
- Use of rage to numb feelings such as shame and hurt (that acknowledge vulnerability) in order to regain a sense of strength and superiority

- An excessive need to exert control over a partner or to withdraw to compensate for inadequate internal management of feelings, i.e., refusing to engage in a discussion of the state of the relationship
- Excessive/inappropriate silliness/joking in serious and emotional situations
- Lack of emotional availability in relationships

3. Relationally deficient self

A pervasive pattern of interpersonal distancing and/or aggressive behaviors resulting in reduced capacity to establish/maintain satisfying, intimate, and enduring relationships:

a. Interpersonal detachment or aggressiveness

- Fear of or discomfort with intimate discussions of common experiences, such as loss or failure, due to inadequate communication skills and/or anxiety about affective statements and self-disclosure
- Defensive autonomy, i.e., reluctance to ask for help when it would clearly be advantageous
- Avoidance of physical contact except in sports, sexual activity, or assaultive behavior
- A pattern of inappropriate competitiveness which interferes with relationships, i.e., an excessive desire to win a board game with a child.

b. Self-protecting inappropriate behaviors

- Overemphasis on hierarchy in relationships and control of others, especially women, to minimize anxiety by using a range of behaviors including physical abuse and manipulation and, in some cases, alternating with exaggerated conciliation and submission

- Preoccupation with activities that provide compensatory satisfaction for inadequacy in relationships and persistent loneliness, i.e., ostentatious displays of wealth, excessive use of social media, and over-competitiveness in team sports
- Obsession with and compulsion about sex as a substitute for intimacy and use of women purely for sexual gratification without regard for their feelings, including paying for sex
- Objectification of women through a range of behaviors from demeaning comments to sexual assault and rape.

It's Just Tough

Mascupathy is a tough disease. Men are taught principles which run counter to their intuitive goodness and their desire to engage with other people. Many remain mascupathic, not because they like it, but because *they don't know any other way.*

Recovery is more grueling than many physical disorders for several reasons. First, although male socialization may explain the origin of the malaise of men, the individual is uniquely responsible for his own recovery. Unlike strep throat, meds alone won't heal mascupathy. Treatment can help: specifically men's therapy groups are effective but, in the psychic inner war, the voices of conventional masculinity are still often loud and the new voices easily drowned out.

Second, recovery is problematic because mascupathy is its own best friend. Like a vine that's resistant to a weed-killer, the roots of male socialization – *just tough it out; don't ever let down your guard; make sure you're always in charge* – undermine men the openness and interdependence necessary for mental health.

Third, mascupathy is an addictive disease. Because it's habitual, recovery becomes increasingly difficult with time. Its patterns of behavior are seductive: dominance over others is compelling; control is gratifying; anger is a high.

Fourth, like life without drugs for the addict, the fear of life without armor is overwhelming for a mascupath. The longer a man is host to the malicious "guest," the more like the guest he becomes. Even when he pushes it out, mascupathy still camps out by the door daily, egging him on, and the temptation is to open the door and let the angry, screaming voices back in. It's tough to heal when you believe your disease is your best friend.

7

Varieties of Mascupathy

Just as men come in all shapes and sizes, their mascupathy emerges in many different ways. One would need, for example, only five seconds to see the difference between Derrick and Steve. Derrick's manner is immediately commanding; he is someone a person would want at her side if she were mountain climbing and a storm came up. Steve, on the hand, has a mushy handshake, but someone could trust him with his life in a completely different way: he'd never reveal one's deepest secret.

As different as they are, Derrick and Steve come from the same place. They happen to be brothers, both work for their dad's business, each is married with two kids. Derrick's an aggressive party guy who cheats on his wife and gets into occasional bar fights. Steve is a homebody who bakes bread and grows herbs in the garden. His wife has to remind him when they haven't had sex for a few weeks. His idea of living it up is having two beers on New Year's Eve.

Both Derrick and Steve harbor weak self-concepts typical of mascupathic men. Although they suffer from similar core symptoms, they experience and express their malaise in different ways. Derrick hides his anxiety with excessive self-confidence and decisiveness while Steve develops resentments and tends to isolate. Both of their families suffer, and neither Derrick nor Steve could be described as a very happy man.

Types of Mascupathic Men

The previous chapter featured the commonalities of mascupathic men. Here are the differences which we've categorized into five types. They describe men who range from acting aggressively to those who passively withdraw, from over-reactivity to relational deficiency.

1. Hypermascupathy

A delusional and grandiose construct of self-importance and entitlement designed to ward off a pervasive sense of powerlessness and not being fully masculine:

- Inadequate awareness of the inner life, i.e., limited consciousness of cognitions, emotions, mood shifts, and limited sensitivity to other's thoughts and feelings
- Unrealistic exaggeration of abilities (especially those associated with traditional masculinity), along with underestimating personal and relational limitations
- Preoccupation with manly activities such as hunting and fishing, aggressive sports, achieving positions of power in business, deification of the male body through musculature, and engagement in exploitive relationships with women such as marriage to a "trophy wife"
- Engagement in power and control tactics such as assault of those who disagree, including domestic abuse of partner
- Pattern of interpersonal exploitation, taking advantage of others without remorse, includes using women for purposes of sexual pleasure only
- A sense of entitlement and unreasonable expectations of others, especially women, to fawn over and serve him, including demands for automatic compliance with wishes and using aggression when compliance is not forthcoming.

Paul was the typical hypermascupathic guy. When his wife, Jean, told him she wanted to fly to Honolulu for her best friend's wedding, he raised his voice and started lecturing, "You always want everything. I got this new job so we can have more money and get a new house, and now you want to waste money on some damn trip two thousand miles away! We can't afford it. You're not going anywhere."

2. Reactive Mascupathy

An unstable personality structure resulting in chronic patterns of mood fluctuation, impulsive behavior, and intermittent, high levels of anxiety about one's masculinity as well as fears of both intimacy and abandonment resulting in overreaction to other's actions:

- Intermittent and fleeting awareness of psychic processes and activities i.e., awareness of feelings of anxiety or significant feelings such as hurt, fear, shame, or joy
- Dogmatic and defensive belief systems that are sometimes paranoid or denigrating to protect self from feelings of fear, powerlessness and insecurity, i.e., the conviction the people who do not meet his needs for affirmation and validation are enemies
- Rapidly changing perceptions of being able to attain traditional masculine status and achievement resulting from boyhood trauma as well as discrepancies between ideals of manhood and ability to meet its unrealistic standards
- Impulsive and sometimes extreme behavior, including emotional or physical attacks on a primary partner or, in extreme cases, random violence
- Frequent vacillations between bellicose and aggressive autonomy and anxious dependence in primary relationships with women alternating between rage and remorse
- Obsession with symbols, activities, and objects, i.e., ostentatious cars or homes, extreme sports, or trophy wives that enliven a fledgling sense of hyper-masculinity.

93

In the intake interview conducted by his therapist, it quickly became evident that Ed's instability started at an early age. As a nine-year-old, he shared he'd regularly get into aggressive and loud arguments with his mother who he thought ignored him, paying too much attention to his siblings. "How come you spend all your time with Jason and Linda? How come you don't care about me?"

He'd slam the door and leave, sometimes staying at his uncle's house rather than be near his mother, who he referred to as "that horrible woman."

After he'd been in the men's group for several months, Ed described a recent encounter with his ex-wife. He was supposed to pick up his four-year-old son, Jimmy, at 5:30 p.m. to take him to McDonald's for dinner. He had to work late, so it was 7:00 p.m. before he arrived at Maureen's house.

Maureen told him that Jimmy had already had dinner and needed to go to bed in an hour – there wasn't time to take him out. Ed was enraged. "You can't tell me that I can't take my son to McDonald's for an ice cream," he bellowed. Jimmy cowered next to his mother as Ed reached out and grabbed the little boy's arm.

Maureen told him not to do that, that he was scaring their son. Then she asked him to leave. "If you keep insisting, I'll call the police."

"You'd call the police on your husband, father of your only son. That's ridiculous!"

There was a moment of silence. "You know, your mother is a real bitch," Ed whispered. "I'll bet you'd rather live with your dad."

Ed squatted so he'd be on the same level as his son. "Jimmy, you'd rather live with me than your mom, wouldn't you?"

Jimmy burst into tears.

"You've got to leave!" Maureen cried.

Ed stood up. "I'm out of here. You'll never see me again." He turned for the door, knocked over a chair, and rushed out.

94

As a reactive mascupath, Ed is among the most difficult of clients. A man with poor ego strength, he often feels victimized. He's mercurial in over-reacting to what he perceives as offenses and manipulative to cover his neediness. Oblivious to the effects he has on others, he lurches through life, one confrontation after another. Ed's problems are so severe that participation in the cognitive resocialization group will not be sufficient, and he'll need to attend a men's experiential group for at least several years. In many aspects of his life Ed gets away with bravado, but in the group, his volatile and combative style will be exposed, and he'll be repeatedly challenged by other group members until he understands and acknowledges the effect of his behavior on others.

3. Relational Deficit Mascupathy

Impairment in men who are otherwise well-adjusted and able to take part in social settings but have difficulty engaging in intimate relationships:

- Inadequate awareness of and ability to express feelings
- Fear of openness and self-disclosure, i.e., sharing faults or risking shame
- Anxiety about competence to speak and act appropriately in intimate settings, i.e., difficulty responding to questions such as, "How do you feel about that?"
- High levels of defensiveness expressed in anger or distancing in response to someone calling attention to the impairment.

A short story: Dog rescues man. *Carl, a seven-year-old, waited to see his dad's Ford truck turn the corner. His dad had promised Carl they'd play catch when he got home. Dad was supposed to be home at 5:30 p.m. and it was now 6:00 p.m., a long time for a little kid. Finally, Carl went into the kitchen and had dinner with his mother and younger sister.*

When his dad arrived at 7:00 p.m., he told Carl, "Sorry, it's almost dark and Dad's really hungry." Tears came to Carl's eyes and his dad said, "Buck up, son." Carl ran into the den and laid his head on their Labrador retriever Molly's soft belly. Molly whipped her tail around in the air; he closed his eyes. For a hurt child, the world warmed up again.

*   *   *   *   *   *   *

Thirty years passed. Carl was now 37 and married with two kids. He and his family lived outside of Albany. Though he'd gotten a B.A. in business administration, Carl always had trouble finding work and had only recently gotten a job as a manager of a clothing store. His boss was a woman, and, at his church, one of the assistant ministers was gay.

Politically centrist, Carl took pride in how he'd adapted to a changing society. Home, though, was often more of a wrangle for him.

Carl's wife, Marge, was the vice-president of marketing at a local bank. Every so often she would tell Carl about her struggles. One night she told him about a trusted employee who'd been caught twice watching baseball on the Internet, and about an advertising company known for its glitzy commercials that wanted to work with the bank. Carl's responses were grandiose and aggressive: "You've got to fire that guy," and, "Don't hire them; they'll ruin your image."

The next day, Carl's brother Richie, sister Lisa, and their spouses came over for dinner. After dinner, Carl started to help clean up in the kitchen, but instead wandered into the den to check the score of the game, sat down on the couch with the other guys and was lost for the night. Later in the evening after the kids were in bed, Marge said, "I need to talk to you." Carl flinched and said, "Now?" as though there were something going on which would have precluded a discussion.

Marge went on: "I've been offered a senior vice president position in Boston." Reflexively, Carl laid down the law: "That's not going to happen. It would be too tough on the kids. Maybe after a couple years … when they're older." Marge responded: "You haven't been engaged in this marriage for a long time. I tell you about stuff at work and you give me lectures when you don't know what you're talking about. You don't spend much time with the kids; I feel like I have to do everything around here."

96

*   *   *   *   *   *   *

A month later, she filed for divorce and took the children with her. Carl was caught completely off-guard. A week after Marge left with their kids, he called his brother. "I need to see you." Dutifully, Richie drove the hundred miles east from Rochester. As the two brothers sat together in the kitchen, Carl said, "I thought she loved me." Richie retorted: "You'll find somebody better than her. I never liked her anyway." Carl closed his eyes and laid his hand on his forehead. In the midst of this painful scene, Carl's chocolate lab, named Molly like his childhood pet, bounded into the room. Carl opened his eyes and pulled the dog close, looked deep into her eyes and gently kissed her on either side of her face. "You are the sweetest dog. Daddy loves you, and you love Daddy."

Carl is not a bad guy – he's certainly not a commando like Paul or volatile like Ed. Carl gets through life okay. He has a reasonable, if uninspiring, job. Yet he exhibits many of the characteristics of mascupathy in general, and of relational deficit mascupathy in particular: self-aggrandizing attempts to dominate his wife, a preference for "side-by-side" interactions with men versus "give-and-take" with women, and transforming his fear that his wife will take a different job into a confrontation and anger. In addition, Carl's dad has taught him the chief lessons of manhood: Don't expect support from other people. So Carl finds solace where he always has: Molly, the dog.

4. Hypomascupathy

A pattern of disturbing internal gender role conflict that appears in two forms.

Ego-syntonic Hypomascupathic Disorder is characterized by a rejection of hyper-mascupathic values and the over-reliance on behaviors typically associated with the feminine that can result in feelings of inadequacy and unsatisfying relationships:

- The presence of wounds from traumatic socialization that lead to an identity antithetical to hyper-masculinity: resistance to competition, personal engagement, and assertiveness as well as

97

the development of a personality structure featuring passivity, timidity, and self-effacement

- Superficial self-knowledge, avoidance of strong feelings, and a desire to control moods and behavior resulting in a depressive temperament in spite of attempts to appear cheerful
- A proclivity for docility, accommodation, and fostering superficial relationships in which both intimacy and healthy confrontation are shunned, behaviors which inevitably lead to unwanted conflict
- Engaging in secretive acting-out behaviors including substance abuse, use of pornography, gambling, and non-relational sex to quell feelings of inadequacy and disappointment.

Tim grew up in a home with a hyper-masculine father and an aggressive brother. The brother bullied him and on several occasions, Tim was present when his father physically battered his mother. At some point during his childhood, Tim went through "reaction formation" a process in which he rejected the toughness associated with conventional masculinity and committed himself to being cheery, friendly, and agreeable, never wanting to hurt or offend anyone.

In the therapy group, Tim's cheerfulness was transparent. He smiled as if it were good news when he reported to the group that his girlfriend was moving to a town a hundred miles away, or that he'd gotten two speeding tickets and if he got another he'd lose his license. When the guys challenged him, Tim said, "Oh, you're right. I know ... I try too hard to be positive. I'm sorry."

Later in the session, when Curtis spoke for the first time of his wife's breast cancer, Tim offered, "Oh, she'll be fine; they have great treatments for breast cancer these days." Curtis flew off the handle, partially because the fear associated with his wife's illness had morphed into anger but also because Tim's attempt to "fix" things was so blatantly inauthentic. Curtis yelled, "You don't get it! You don't get anything at all!" Though Tim had worked on his hypomascupathy in group for a year, he was still stunned by Curtis' outburst.

Ego-dystonic Hypomascupathic Disorder is typified by the presence of feminine characteristics inconsistent with a strong but failed attempt to incorporate masculine qualities:

- The presence of high levels of internal conflict, anxiety, and self-recrimination that stems from the exhibiting of feminine qualities or absence of manly characteristics viewed as inconsistent with masculinity
- Extreme interest in objects or hobbies such as gun or knife collecting and violent video games, to buoy a fledgling masculine identity
- A pattern of unstable, short-term, and/or abusive relationships leading to feelings of inadequacy and a sense of victimization
- The use of passive-aggressive behavior such as manipulative deference and over-politeness interspersed with occasional compulsive acting-out behaviors such as belligerence and assault to compensate for perceptions of inadequacy.

Stan grew up in a military family and throughout his life struggled with his perceived failures of not measuring up as a man. Like many ego-dystonic hypomascupaths, he was shy and nervous as a child. Stationed at various military posts, Stan was ridiculed as the gangly new guy each time his family moved. He finally landed at a small school, so he thought that this time he might make the baseball team. He didn't, while his younger brother Bill went on to be a star pitcher.

Stan found solace in science fiction and literature. His father, a controlled man, did not reprove him for what he felt were feminine pursuits, but simply wrote him off.

Stan did well in school and enrolled in a small college, going on to get a Ph.D. in English literature and finding a tenure track position at a state university. He married Linda, a successful real estate agent. He worked hard as a professor, but his anxiety and poor social skills were obstacles to effective teaching and his student evaluations were often poor.

Though Stan's father marveled at Bill's station as a circuit court judge and his stories of court room drama, he'd occasionally and absent-mindedly ask Stan, "So, did you say you got tenure yet?"

At home, Stan often stayed up late grading papers in a blur of bourbon. Linda threatened to leave him if he didn't stop his drinking. At the end of his fourth year, the department chair advised Stan that the tenure committee had voted against tenure. Mortified, he couldn't imagine having to tell Linda and his parents about yet another failure to measure up. He went home, got his handgun, and drove back to the university with a plan to burst into a departmental meeting. When he arrived, he found he just couldn't bring himself to do it. Instead he checked himself into a motel, lay in bed, drank a fifth of bourbon, and took a half a bottle of Valium. The maid found him a couple hours later, and called 911. After his discharge from a psychiatric hospital, Stan arrived at a men's counseling center.

Although Stan did not carry out his intentions, he came close to killing those he believed responsible for his troubles and taking his own life to end his suffering. Stan is proof that some shooters – probably most – are not hypermascupathic but hypomascupathic. Whereas hypermascupaths enjoy exhibiting exaggerated masculinity, hypomascupathic men engage in externalized behavior to counter a self-perception of inadequate manhood. John Lee, in *Half Lived Life*, offers this analysis: "Passive people are usually full of rage; in large part because they feel other people and life itself have refused them in multiple ways."

PART IV
Healing

8

Resocialization Training

Though ordinary psychotherapies can sometimes be effective for men, our experience is that they make greater and more long-lasting transformations in a tiered sequence of men's treatment, therapy, and support groups. The Resocialization, Reclamation, and Recovery protocol is a three-stage program to facilitate men's understanding of mascupathic disorder, ameliorate its symptoms, and find a sense of self most haven't experienced since childhood.

Phase One, Resocialization Training, utilizes male gender-specific cognitive therapies in structured groups to challenge men's core belief systems – *I'm a guy, and I've got to be tough* – and open their minds to alternative ways of thinking such as *I'm a guy, and I can be assertive rather than aggressive.* The process features this first step: acknowledging harmful behaviors such as distancing, control, and condescension as well as externalizing bad feelings with substances, excessive sex or rage, and emotional or physical abuse in intimate relationships. Men also learn to replace grandiosity and rationalization with clear and accountable thinking, increase awareness of the consequences of their behavior, and expand their capacity for empathy.

Phase Two, Experiential Reclamation Therapy, continues the process of resocialization but employs male-specific psychotherapeutic group activities that guide men to rediscover the balances of childhood lost to rigid socialization including trust, self-revelation, and easy intimacy.

Phase Three, Recovery, is a lifelong pursuit, like rehabilitation from addictions. The ultimate goal is to create an integrated life – incorporating the best qualities traditionally associated with the masculine and the feminine.

This chapter explains Resocialization Training. The next chapter describes both the Experiential Reclamation group and Recovery, the aftercare program. Before talking about Resocialization, here are a few reasons why group work for men is preferred over individual therapy, and a comment about the difficulties of creating a therapeutic alliance with men.

Advantages of group work. Over the years, we've worked with men in individual counseling, couples therapy, and group work, and found group therapy to be far and away the most effective for three reasons:

- The source of a man's problems is often found in the company of men; the company of men is also the solution. Men's groups harness the ancient energy of the pack – the desire to belong – for relational and accountable outcomes. Guys who've been in a group longer model taking off the mask of mascupathy and admit bad behaviors and weaknesses; they also model accountability and openness. Once newcomers sense they are welcomed and find they won't be judged, they are quick to follow the elders' lead.
- The group is a safe arena for practicing new behaviors. A man who acts out in group – for example, ridiculing another group member – can learn to practice de-escalation, and then use this newly acquired tool in his primary relationship and other real-life settings.
- Beyond presenting more opportunities to interact, groups provide the therapist with numerous occasions to observe a client's behavior. How a man behaves in group is a good indication of how he behaves in his life in general – providing a broader and deeper view than one-on-one treatment.

While individual counseling pales in comparison to the vibrant colors of the microcosm of the men's group, it does have a place in our treatment plans as a supportive service in which the client can process what's happened in group in more detail and explore personal issues at greater length.

The therapeutic alliance. It's axiomatic that therapists need to develop an alliance with clients to promote insight and healing. Built on a relationship of unconditional positive regard, clients reveal wounds and express difficult feelings. In addition, issues that arise in the group often reflect problems experienced in the larger world, and examining them in group can lead to more enlightened behavior elsewhere.

> *In the group, Ralph found himself agitated and angry at Troy's loud voice. He explored his reactions and, with help from the group, discovered that Troy reminded him of his intimidating older brother. In life, Ralph had feared confronting his brother, but in the safe environment of the group he could analyze and discuss his response with Troy, an open-heartedness he'd never before experienced.*

While the therapist trained in mascupathic treatments provides a milieu of acceptance and trust, he also establishes clear boundaries and is more frequently confrontational than in other therapeutic approaches. For example, men frequently invite therapists to "join" with them in degrading their partners and blaming them for their relationship problems. The client's message is, *"Because you're a guy, you should support me in my conflict with my wife."* Therapists refuse to collude, explaining that disparaging comments are not allowed. The therapist's job is not to support mascupathic behavior of placing culpability on a partner, but to help men take responsibility for their behaviors and to correct them.

Transforming Beliefs

Beliefs are the scripts we live by that unconsciously dictate our behavior – the thoughts behind our thoughts. Male socialization teaches a myriad of beliefs, some of which are helpful while others undermine health and relationships. Resocialization groups challenge conventional beliefs and offer alternatives.

Hierarchical Belief: *I make the money, so I should decide how it's spent.*
Egalitarian Belief: Everybody has an important role in our home.

Patriarchal Belief: *I'm a guy, and I have rights.*
Personal Power: I have the right to ask for what I want, but others have rights, too.

Male Privilege: *I get together with the guys at the bar, and she puts the kids to bed.*
Fairness: We share responsibilities.

Aggression: *The world's a harsh place; you have to be tough out there.*
Conciliation: Things go better if I calm down, reflect options, and join in finding solutions.

Invulnerability: *Real men don't let anything get to them.*
Vulnerability: Real relationships happen when people are open-hearted and may involve disappointment and hurt.

Distancing: *When things don't go my way, I'm out of there.*
Engagement: When I don't get what I want, I hang in there and look for commonality.

Anti-social Behaviors

In response to a rash of domestic violence in Duluth, Minnesota in 1981, the Domestic Abuse Intervention Project (DAIP) pioneered a treatment approach from which we developed Resocialization Training. We use Resocialization Training when working with externalization symptoms of mascupathy such as substance abuse, sex addiction, and domestic violence.

While some anti-social behaviors stem from malevolence, domestic abuse often grows out of emotional illiteracy, inadequate intimacy skills, a sense of entitlement – "I've got some rights" – and a tendency to act out to gain control in emotionally-laden conflicts. Domestic abuse exemplifies the core characteristics of mascupathy and is legitimized by a still-prevalent acceptance of male privilege and patriarchy.

Below is Liam's account of his experience in a resocialization group session that challenged his belief system and made him sit back and take a good look at his life.

Without warning, about eight months ago, Jenny and the kids moved out. I knew sometimes I got pissed off, but it didn't seem so bad that she'd leave me. I came home from work to an empty house: their clothes and a lot of furniture and stuff were gone.

The only person left in the house to look in the mirror was me. I just wandered around in circles, ate at McDonald's, and zoned out watching the stupid summer Olympics. I didn't even know how to get a hold of Jenny, but finally I found out where she was. She told me flat out that there was only one chance of us getting back together: I had to go to this Domestic Relations Accountability Group to learn to stop being abusive. I thought, "What a bunch of crap. She was the problem. She was the one who got upset so easily."

Anyway, I started attending the group. There were ten other guys, mostly referred by the courts. I looked around the room and thought, "What a bunch of losers." The group facilitator, Stuart, explained that the group was about accountability, and I thought, "This is so much crap. This group isn't for me. I'm a responsible guy. I work hard at my job and pay my bills on time. I never got arrested for anything. I don't even drink."

A few weeks later, Stuart explained that we were going to talk about responsible parenting. I thought, "This is going to be easy. I love my kids, and I'd never hit them. I go to John's soccer games and take Leslie to ballet lessons."

In the go-round, Stuart asked each guy to tell the group about his kids — their names and what they liked to do. He also asked each guy if he had ever abused his kids, and if thought he was a good parent. When my turn came, I told him John was seven and Leslie was nine and about all the stuff I did with them. He asked me if I yelled at Jenny and ever hit her. I hemmed and hawed but I knew I had to come clean. I admitted I had done both of those things.

After each guy had talked about his kids, Stuart asked us to raise our hands if we thought we were good dads. Everybody, including me, raised his hand. Then Stuart wrote something on the white board: "Kids identify totally with their mother. They feel everything she feels. If you have abused her, they've felt her pain, so you've abused your kids too. And, you're a bad dad."

Stuart read what he'd written three times, slowly. There was a long uncomfortable silence. Then he said, "Abusing your partner wipes out all the good stuff you do with your kids. It's like it hasn't happened at all."

I felt like I'd gotten the wind kicked out of me. I looked down at my lap; I couldn't look at the other guys to see what was going on with them. But I'm sure it was the same as with me. That was the start of me realizing I was an asshole. And that was the start of me realizing I'd have to change a lot of things in myself to be a good husband and dad.

Resocialization groups use client self-disclosure, group conscience, and provocative and challenging didactics (teaching) with men who need accountability training. Beyond that, they sometimes use confrontation and mild manipulation. Stuart's group tactics caught the men off guard, forcing them to recognize a truth about themselves that otherwise might not have had as much impact.

Structured Activities

The Resocialization Training Group is, compared to the therapy group, highly structured. In a therapy group, issues flow spontaneously, from personal experiences group members bring to the group and interactions between members, whereas resocialization training is like a class with a planned agenda. The facilitator uses structured activities such as worksheets to engage clients. For example, many accountability groups – substance abuse, batterer intervention, and anger management – use a worksheet sometimes called the Alternative Behaviors Log (ABL), modeled from the DAIP Control Log. This exercise employs cognitive-behavioral approaches to examine erroneous core beliefs and identify distorted thinking habits such as denial and rationalization.

More specifically, the ABL is the single most powerful resocialization tool from which our clients learn:

- Behavior is instrumental: their choice of threatening or humiliating actions is not accidental; it is purposeful, usually to gain control
- The first step of accountability is acknowledging hurtful behavior and the harm it causes others
- Empathy forestalls bad behavior
- Bad behavior can be replaced with alternative actions that will often accomplish intentions without harming others.

Many men come to resocialization groups so deficient in introspection that they seldom consider alternate behaviors. Group members may fill out and explain 15 or 20 ABLs over the course of six to 12 months in the group. Repeated use of ABLs opens them to recognizing they have choices. (On the following page is a sample ABL in which a client discusses an incident from the previous week.)

For some men, however, cognitive resocialization doesn't go deep enough. They have powerful feelings that lie underneath their beliefs: fears of abandonment, shame over inadequacy, anxiety that amorphous bad things will happen.

To counter uncomfortable feelings, many men create an inflated view of themselves, blaming others for their problems (narcissism) to counter fears of inadequacy to handle life events. Other men distance themselves from other people out of fear of rejection.

Resocialization Training can help to expose these fears and their compensatory personality styles, but all too often these forces are beyond the purview of cognitive therapy. Therefore, many men who have completed Resocialization Training are encouraged to enter Experiential Reclamation Therapy.

ALTERNATIVE BEHAVIORS LOG
Name: Herman Meyer
Date: 2/28/14

1. What was the situation?
Maria wanted to visit her mother who was just home from the hospital last Friday evening.

2. What did you do to control your partner?
I told her that she should spend Friday evening with me; she could see her mother the next day. I told her everything else was always more important than me. When she got her things and started for the door I grabbed her wrist and forced her to sit down. She started crying. Then, I said, "OK, you can go."

3. What was your intention?
I wanted to let her know that I was supposed to come first, that I was the boss, and that bad things could happen if she didn't treat me right. I wanted us to have sex on a Friday night.

4. What was the impact of the behavior? On her/you?
She was angry, afraid, and hurt. She lost trust in me. The next day, I felt like a jerk, and I was scared she'd leave me.

5. How could you have handled this differently?
Remember that I'm not the only person in her universe, and that sometimes of course her mother would be more important than me. Remind myself that just because I have feelings of insecurity doesn't mean I should always get what I want, and it's my job to deal with my insecurities and not coerce her into doing something to make them go away. I could have taken a time-out or called somebody in the group. Also, I could have gone with her for a short visit with her mom, and we would still have had plenty of time together after we got home.

9

Reclamation and Recovery

The fields of modern medicine, psychiatry, and psychology have their roots in the latter half of the nineteenth and beginning of the twentieth centuries. Theories of disease and treatment were developed by men who were physicians and scientists with sharp powers of observation and analytic minds, probably not people who viewed relationships as particularly significant. They were also typically individualistic, upstanding and respected members of their communities who most likely did not struggle with loneliness and estrangement. These thinkers and scientists lived in a time when self-reliance was lauded, and the world of self-disclosure and intimacy, if existent, were minor aspects of life. Hence, their theories emphasized individual physical and psychic problems rather than difficulties in interpersonal relationships.

The identification and inclusion of disorders of the mind in the canon of diseases came somewhat later than did physical ailments. When psychiatrists (physicians of the psyche) developed the list of disorders in the *DSM*, they followed the pattern of physical disorders listed in the International Statistical Classification of Diseases and Related Health Problems. Using the medical model, their categorization of individuals' minds and behavior excluded factors such as relationship as the source of human problems. In addition, since virtually all of these pioneers were men, their own mascupathy probably obscured their perceptions so they saw traditional feminine characteristics – such as dependence – as pathological, failing to address truly aberrant male traits like the proclivity for violence.

This confluence of attitudes and events led to poor vision in the study of male psychology. *What contributed most to this limited vision was the perception that symptoms such as anxiety and depression and consequent behavioral problems were the product of deranged psyches in contrast to the malady of inadequate relationality.* Traditional professionals in our field asserted that psychological problems come first and create poor relationships. What we have seen repeatedly with the clients in our practices is that it's poor relationships – or none at all – which lead to anxiety and depression. While we certainly address specific disorders such as various forms of trauma and family of origin issues, we find that emphasis on the here and now of relationships brings far greater progress.

Our program, Experiential Reclamation Therapy, utilizes men's experience of their relationships in *men's therapy groups* to reclaim the joy, tenderness, and transparency of childhood. As men progress through the group process, they are transformed because, perhaps for the first time since they were young boys, they find a place of safe relationality. In contrast to the rest of their lives, men in groups can spontaneously express themselves without the competitiveness and ridicule so common to men's experience; they let down their guard, finding the courage of self-disclosure, the generosity of acceptance, the resolution of shame, and the incorporation of self-compassion.

The advantages of group work. Men's therapy groups create a lifelike environment full of interactions with other men, but also provide an alternative universe. Gone is the jockeying for position, and in its place, mutuality and acceptance.

Individual work, the traditional treatment of choice for men, is limited to interactions between the therapist and the client. It's like a couple guys kicking a soccer ball back and forth: limited roles and room for relationship. Men's groups are like a soccer match – something's always happening in a group and roles change constantly. The other advantage of group work is that, like a soccer team that analyzes the game afterward, men's groups are regularly self-examining. Here's a scene from one of our groups:

Dan was talking about a recent encounter with his dad in which he once again attempted to make a real connection. Dan

116

said he told him, "Dad, you know I used to think that you were just mean when you pushed me so hard in sports and everything, but since I've been in this men's group I've realized that you were just doing what you thought was right." Dan said his dad looked him in the eye for just a moment then turned and walked away without a word.

Jordan looked at Dan, and started to say something when Marty, new to the group, blurted out, "Why in hell do we always have to talk about our dads? I mean, everybody keeps saying the same thing. It's a waste of time."

Silence descended on the room, but inside the guys, there was plenty happening.

Ned leaned forward in his chair. "Marty, I know you think it's a waste of time. Let me tell you something about me. For a long time, I thought some of the guys in group were just whiners. Then Jules, a guy who graduated a couple years ago, told me that I was getting pissed off at what some other guy in the group was saying because it was exactly what I needed but least wanted to hear. I'm guessing that if it makes you nervous and angry, you really just don't want to think about your dad."

"That's crap," Marty said.

Simon, the therapist, entered the conversation. "Marty, we're here to support each other. Just take a deep breath."

"Why in hell should I take a deep breath? I'm breathing just fine."

For some time no one spoke. Then Simon continued, "How about if you tell us about your dad. You haven't even mentioned him in this group."

Marty looked down in his lap for a long time as though studying how to fix some small machine. Finally, he looked up and gazed at Dan. "O.K. I'll tell you something. My dad went to work one day, and never came home. He just never came home. I was fourteen. I couldn't believe it. I couldn't talk to anybody for a week. I refused to go to school. Finally my mother sent me to this shrink, and he was a jerk. He told me that happened to lots of kids, and I'd just have to deal with it.

117

Deal with it! What the hell does that mean? Five years later, when I'm nineteen, we find out he lives across the country and has a new wife. Except he never divorced my mother."

Again there was silence, but this time the men were breathing easier. Finally, the therapist looked at Marty and said, "Look up at the guys in this room. Look at their eyes. What do you see?"

"I don't see anything."

Jordan's voice was low and his words came out slowly. "Marty, none of us had our fathers walk out, never to come back. That's terrible. But we've all had dads who, for one reason or another, hurt us. And the bad thing is that we lost our trust in other people, especially other men."

"That's right," Ned said, "We stopped trusting, and we started to walk the world alone. But in this group, we're learning to trust each other. If you look at the eyes, you can see it, the softness. When I first met Dan and Jordan, I thought they were idiots. It's been a couple years, but I've learned to trust them. Sometimes in this group we get pissed at each other, but I'd trust these guys with my life. And so now I trust people outside of this group a little more. You can have that too. Just give the group a chance."

The power of the pack. The source of men's problems, and also the solution, rests within the pack. The new pack has turned the old rules upside down. Look at what happened in the group. Marty was a frightened guy – afraid of the group, fearful of his own feelings. He attacks because that makes him feel safer, and, instead of attacking back, the group responds with gentle words and soothing. It may take years, but Marty will come around.

In *Tough Guise*, Katz shows a clip from the film *Varsity Blues* in which a player complains of the pain in his knee. The coach remonstrates him, *"Never show weakness, never show weakness. The only pain that matters is the pain you inflict."* The message is clear: Men should never confess physical or emotional pain. The only manly feeling is anger, and it's okay to express that one loud and often.

Stop to think about this: it's phenomenal how infrequently men actually speak from their hearts. Perhaps at a funeral or when their partner pushes them into it, but seldom spontaneously. Wearing unemotional armor to stay manly is a common attribute among men; in the alternative world of the men's groups, shedding that armor is a requirement. Marty's interactions with Ned and Jordan helped him see that he needed to lay down his armor in order to heal and progress.

The gift of the elders. It's the elders, the guys who've been in the group for several years, who have created a safe place without the hierarchy, ridicule, and derision that had been their calling cards for many years. They've learned that what men want more than anything else is simple acceptance: *"I understand. I know just how you feel."*

Therapists hold back and let the elders pass the torch. Elders know what it's like when the group really works, as when Jordan and Ned modeled self-disclosure and accountability in speaking quiet, compassionate words. They've been there in those remarkable times when the connection in the room is palpable, when defenses fall away, when, without prompting or even awareness, every man speaks more softly and slowly than usual. The tone of men's voices, in those moments, is as important as the meaning of the words.

Time slows down when intimacy happens; small exchanges that would otherwise go unnoticed are examined in detail. Comments that elsewhere might be ridiculed are addressed sensitively. That doesn't mean that there's never any conflict in group. What it *does* mean is that when there are difficult moments these men are less likely to posture and more likely to manage difficult feelings and resolve discord.

For newer members like Marty, the elders can be the loving older brother most boys never had. Instead of teaching them the secrets of sex with girls before they were really ready, or callously taunting them into toughness, the elder offers a new form of relationship.

The intimacy of the elders is initially alien and frightening, even more frightful than life in general. New group members feel as if they're venturing into a foreign land where they don't know the language. In fact, when Dan spoke of his pain about his father and Ned and Jordan reached out to Marty, they were doing what comes naturally – what they did as boys before the man-pack scolded and intimidated them into believing they shouldn't be real. The men in the group – grown, competent, and successful males – have reclaimed some of the sweetness of boyhood intimacy. They haven't turned back into children; they've simply found wonder and easy connection and brought it into their adult lives.

The here and now. While most therapy focuses on what happened last week – for example, a troubling interaction a guy had with his wife – Experiential Reclamation Therapy focuses on what's happening in group in real time.

What's important in Marty's experience in group is not actually that he revealed the painful story of being deserted by his father; it's the opportunity to see himself and let others see him. When men who attend these groups feel safe enough to be transparent, every interaction becomes an opportunity to look behind the mask. Men in group ask and answer questions like these: *Why did Marty get so angry at Dan when he tried to bond with his dad? Why is it so hard to look other men in the eye, and when a man does it, why does he miss the softness of the other man's eyes? When it's his turn to check-in, why does Marty still feel like running for the door?*

Guys fall in love with their group. The couple of hours they spend each week fully living in the present is transformative: men come alive in their groups – the unfocused becomes clear, low energy morphs into high spirits, isolation is replaced with community.

The Lost Region of Men's Lives

For centuries, human beings' inner experience has been described as having four components: cognition, emotion, physicality, and spirituality. Of the many dehumanizing instructions males receive as they are being socialized as boys, the single most damaging instruction is to not have emotions. Feelings are for women and children. Feelings get in the way of getting things done; they interrupt task-oriented thinking, muddy the waters, and make men soft in battle and powerless in relationships.

Since most men erect a wall between feelings and consciousness and therefore don't experience much of an inner life, they simply believe they don't have any feelings. Despite their inattentiveness to their inner lives and efforts to ignore what is happening, their interior world continues to function and, sometimes, their emotions overwhelm them.

When Dwight first started with the group, he said he considered himself to be "kind of autistic." Actually, the therapist thought that was an excuse, but he let it go because Dwight was already a very defensive man. Dwight added that he didn't pride himself on not having feelings; he simply convinced himself that he just wasn't built to have any. But when he revealed another group member's secret, that he'd been imprisoned for selling drugs, to someone outside of the group, Dwight was confronted by the other group members for violating confidentiality, and he was clearly humiliated.

Immediately on the defense, Dwight minimized his behavior and instinctively turned his embarrassment into anger at the group: "Why are you making such as big deal out of this?" which triggered more confrontation from the group and more shame for Dwight. Over the next several weeks, Dwight and the whole group spent hours processing this important event.

Though Dwight eventually admitted his mistake and recognized his shame, he also thereafter distanced himself from the other group members. His self-reports in the check became even more cerebral; his responses to other group members seemed practiced and stilted. The group repeatedly reached out to him and the therapist worked with him in individual sessions, but Dwight's heart had shut down. After another six months, he simply stopped showing up. He didn't return voicemails or texts.

A chart of feelings. Guys certainly know that "things bother" them, but that fuzzy description doesn't address their real feelings of despair, suspicion, and apathy. Many men are so emotionally unaware that it's common for therapists to use The Feelings Chart – a long list of emotions such as hurt, disappointment, disgrace, and elation, each with a picture of the facial expression associated with that feeling. In the men's group, Mort said:

121

When I saw my old college buddy at a reunion, he told me it didn't seem like we had much in common anymore." Somebody in the group asked him, "So, how do you feel about that?" Mort responded, "Well, it certainly made me feel bad." Joel said, "I guess it's time to get out the feeling chart." The guys smiled sympathetically; they had all been there before.

The tandem of *don't feel* and *don't talk about it* creates a lethal alienation among men. Daniel Goleman's 1995 book, *Emotional Intelligence*, is nearly 20 years old, and in spite of its popularity, Goleman's simple message – that Emotional Quotient is a better predictor of success in life than Intelligence Quotient – is still lost on most men. In another important tome, *Thinking in the Shadow of Feelings: A New Understanding of the Hidden Forces that Shape Individuals and Societies*, psychiatrist Reuven Bar Levav recognized that feelings distort thinking. The goal is for men to make room for feelings, but not let feelings rule their lives.

Escape into Intimacy

At its core, mascupathy is a disease of impaired relationship, of distance and rejection. Here's the account of David's escape from the dark tunnel he'd made for himself long ago.

The group was in extended session, a daylong retreat. Several group members had already participated in role-plays that sparked breakthroughs for other men. Now David was finally ready to take a turn. A handsome man in his forties with an abundant crop of amber hair, he was a successful contractor, well-known and respected in his community. But David had also struggled in group, sometimes even mocking the process and rejecting the invitations of other men to open up.

This afternoon, however, he started off by telling the men, "This is a birthday in my life. It was thirty years ago today that my mom finally kicked my dad out of the house, and he actually left. I never saw him again."

The therapist looked at David and then at the men in the circle, all eyes on their fellow group member. "You were a scared, lonely kid. You didn't tell anybody about it. So what did you do?"

For the first time, David began to reveal himself. "I'd hide in a little closet under the stairs to the basement. Dad would go to the bar after work and get home pretty drunk. He'd come looking for me but he never found me down there. He was too drunk, and he'd think I was still out with my friends."

"But you didn't have any friends. You'd just go to your safe place."

"I even took in a pillow, some blankets, a couple books."

"David, don't you think you <u>still</u> spend a lot of time hiding under the stairs?"

David nodded. The therapist explained that David continued to disappear into his little room of mascupathy, that even though he'd participated in both the resocialization group and this group, he still sometimes withdrew from the group in silence and other times came out with verbal head-butts, attacking the other guys in the group. Deciding to use psychodrama, the therapist proposed they replicate the hiding place closet David had retreated to over three decades ago. The other guys set up six big upholstered chairs with a space in the middle to make a small room against the wall.

* * * * * * *

"David, so is this like the place under the stairs?"

"Well, I'm a lot bigger now."

The guys laughed. "We know that."

"Where'd you sit?"

"I'd sit with my back against the wall, and pull my legs up into my chest, and then put my arms around my legs to make myself into a little ball."

"Can you go into the closet and make yourself into that little ball?"

David got on his hands and knees, crawled between the chairs, and pulled his big body tight together. The other guys sat on the floor around the closet. "So, just sit there and remember what it

123

was like." The therapist paused. "What did you think about when you were in there?"

"I thought how much I hated him. I prayed he'd die. I was so depressed I didn't have any friends. I was so alone so much of the time. It was terrible."

"David, I want you to say, 'I can't stand it. I'm just so lonely.' I want you to say those two sentences quietly over and over."

"I can't stand it. I'm just so lonely." "I can't stand it. I'm just so lonely." As he repeated these sentences, the men could hear his initial tone of anger change to sadness. Gradually, the tears came and turned into sobs until they could barely make out the words, but he didn't stop. Sitting around him in his closet, some of the guys were crying, too.

*   *   *   *   *   *   *

The therapist let this go on for several minutes until he sensed David is spent. "O.K., you can stop now, David. Your dad's gone now, and you don't have to hide any more. You don't have to believe the world outside the closet is a dangerous place. You have friends now. Look around. See the guys. It's safe here."

David glanced up, shuddered, and started to cry again. Through his tears, he was smiling slightly, taking in the affirming faces of the circle of men around him. It was as if he were thinking to himself, "It's true. I have friends now."

"These guys like you, David. They want you to come out now. Are you ready to do that?"

David crawled slowly out between the chairs.

The therapist motioned the guys to sit around David, to nestle in a circle close to him. They placed their hands on his neck, shoulders, back, and legs. The therapist asked David to repeat, "You are my friends now, and I don't have to hide anymore," until he told him to stop. Gradually, David's tears were no longer about pain but gratitude. He smiled. The other men in the group didn't say anything. David could see in their faces everything he needed to know.

Like David, most men in groups are able to break down the walls that have closeted their emotional lives. And although not every man in every group ends up in tears, tears are often the expression of relief and joy. When David crawled out of his closet, each of them, in their own way, found a new sense of safety and connection – the start of a new day.

Recovery

As with addiction, there is no cure for mascupathy, only remission. Men can learn to be respectful and even selfless, but they will always have to be watchful of their psyches. Similar to long-term substance abuse treatment, Resocialization Training and Experiential Reclamation Therapy groups provide a strong foundation, but long-term allegiance to liberated masculinity requires permanent commitment. Like alcoholic relapse, mascupathy is like a serpent waiting in the bushes: cunning, baffling, and patient, ready to prey on the man who stumbles, who drops his guard, who isn't vigilant about maintaining the balanced life.

One of A.A.'s many homey sayings is, "If you hang around a barbershop long enough, sooner or later you'll get a haircut," referring to the probability of relapse not only for folks who still go to bars and drink Coke, but also people who aren't working the A.A. program. Just as recovering alcoholics continue to need to attend A.A., so mascupathic men will greatly enhance the probability of permanent recovery with attendance of a support group. Such groups are generally leaderless, established by men who have completed therapist-directed treatment.

While there are parallels between recovery from alcoholism and mascupathy, in some ways rehabilitation from mascupathy is more challenging.

Ron had six years of abstinence from alcohol, but he'd just lost a major client and was upset. Sitting in an airport restaurant with three hours to kill before his flight, Ron ordered a whiskey sour and then four more. He slept it off on the plane, waking up in his home city enraged at himself for what he'd done. There was no question in his mind that he'd relapsed. He knew he needed to call his sponsor right away and get to a bunch of A.A. meetings fast.

Unlike recovery from alcoholism, when you clearly know when you've had a drink, abstinence from mascupathy is not a clearly delineated event. Slipping into active mascupathy can be subtle as well as obvious. Triggers (events that lead to relapse) for the man in recovery from mascupathy are less definable and more frequent than those for the alcoholic: the toxicity of other mascupathic men who play a rough game of king-of-the-mountain in sales planning meetings, who cut off other drivers on the freeway, who ridicule other men's sex lives at the bar. Even a small remonstration at the kitchen table – "You haven't done anything around this house all week" – can trigger a relapse. Alcoholics can avoid places such as bars and parties where people are drinking, but mascupathic trigger situations strike without warning.

Art came home and found that Rachel had bought five hundred dollars' worth of fabric for new window treatments. He immediately recognized this as a relapse situation and reminded himself: "Quiet voice, low tones, careful words, breathe." But when Rachel said, "You bought a new yard tractor; window curtains seem like a relatively small expense," Art's mascupathy escalated. "Don't you want me to mow the damn lawn?" he asked her in a too-loud voice. Not a full-blown relapse, but big enough that Rachel retreated into herself and conversation was awkward for the next couple of days.

At A.A. they make a distinction between abstinence and sobriety. Abstinence is self-enforced – you avoid the use of alcohol on your own, white-knuckling it. For people who do it alone, relapse is almost expected. For those who choose sobriety, the prospects are much improved. Sobriety is not just a goal; it's a way of life. The process for alcoholics includes more than sitting at the table of A.A. meetings frequently; it also includes checking in daily with a sponsor-mentor and working through the Twelve Steps.

While a broader recovery management program from mascupathy has yet to be developed, men need support groups.

Not to whine or complain, but to gain solace that they are not alone in their struggles and to identify and challenge each other's problematic thoughts and actions.

As we move deeper into the 21st century, men's issues are getting attention from a society that has historically operated with the assumption that guys will be guys. While the trek from mascupathy to men's liberation is still more like sparks than the steady beam of a spotlight, the light grows brighter as more men come together to save their psychic and relational lives. A few years ago, Hanna Rosin titled her book *The End of Men*. In a rapidly-changing world, the title is already out of date. Today the story is one we call *Men's New Beginning*.

10

Societal Change toward a New Masculinity

Although men such as Ned and David make significant turns in their lives, the number of men who engage in treatment is relatively small. In spite of the increasing willingness of men to attend counseling and new court mandates for men convicted of domestic violence and driving/drinking offenses, treatment alone will only make a small dent in eliminating the problem of mascupathy on a societal level.

A quick glance at the landscape does not present encouragement about the social transformation of men. In fact, an article in the December 2013 issue of *The Atlantic* buttresses the notion that, in the world of gender role change, women are center-stage while men are still in the wings. In the piece by Heather Horn and Svati Kirsten Narula, "The Great American Gender Debates of 2013," seven of the 11 examples tell the stories of transition in women's rights and roles, including: "Women Who Opt Out," "Sex and the College Girl," "Women Will Fill Combat Roles," and "Get Better Procedures for Reporting Sexual Assault." The only one about men, "Marriage Is Good for Your Career – If You're a Man," straddles the fence on the issue of men, matrimony, and work.

Indeed, on a macro scale, the path to a new masculinity is probably more difficult than the development of a new feminism. The reason is simple: When you're on the outside, marginalized and perhaps victimized, you have considerable motivation to change society to redress your lower status. Women, for example, have found stronger voices and propelled their way into positions of influence formerly in the reins of men – from Supreme Court justices to CEOs of major corporations such as General Motors. Most men, however, still hold positions of considerably greater power. When you've got the spoils, you don't have much motivation to change.

Under the Radar. So, is the idea of a wider transformation – something that could encompass all men that would somehow make them kinder and gentler – a possibility or fantasy? In spite of men's resistance, *we believe that much in fact is happening to men, but it is still under the radar.*

Although the emergence of a new masculinity certainly lags behind the development of feminism, we nevertheless see a cultural insurgency that's gaining strength. For example, in some couples, women and men alternate roles with an ease that couldn't have been imagined just a couple decades ago. There are no set rules about who's in the driver's seat – literally and metaphorically. It's increasingly common for a father to work at home while the mother works in the office. And men are quietly changing how they act with other men: offering up a hug instead of a slap on the back, sitting beside one another at a restaurant instead of across the table, and sharing concerns about aging parents instead of just football highlights.

Here are descriptions of two very different types of organizations which suggest that the momentum toward new men in a new millennium emanates from both expected and unexpected places. One group of organizations liberates men by design, with an overt mission to change men and manhood. The other group includes stalwartly mascupathic entities, each of which has its own goals which are unrelated to male gender role change, but has begun to support men's transformation with its message. These organizations have discovered that to succeed they can be more effective when they replace conventional masculine approaches with methods and messages similar to those we use in our treatment programs. Inadvertently, they further the cause of creating more open and responsive men.

Liberating Men by Intent

Men have been joining together to support the emancipation of women and male gender role development for at least a century. Floyd Dell, a prophet of men's liberation, wrote in 1914, "It is feminism that will truly set men free," and his prophecy is becoming a reality. One hundred years later, it is women's independence and rejection of conventional roles that challenge men to broaden their own roles.

Since the 1970s, various groups have been intentional, principled, and persistent in promoting change. While not publicized in the mainstream media, here are some that are representative of this societal change by design.

Profeminists. For nearly two generations, a growing number of men of all races and ethnicities have set the specific goal of preventing domestic violence and sexual violence, as well as redefining male gender roles. Rob Okun, author of the 2014 book *VOICE MALE: The Untold Story of the Profeminist Men's Movement* and the editor of *Voice Male* magazine, writes, "Profeminist men hold the simple 'radical' belief that gender and sexual equality are fundamental democratic goals, and that women and men should each have the same rights and opportunities."

Boys to Men (B2M) Mentoring. Founded in 1996 in San Diego, California, B2M is a model for community-based mentoring. Its vision is to encourage boys to become compassionate, accountable men by providing communities of men who teach, support, and inspire them. B2M provides mentors at middle schools, high schools, and foster care facilities. Regular meetings provide boys, many of whom are growing up without a father, the opportunity to meet with men who consistently show up to tell the truth about their struggles as men, praise the boys for their abilities, and support them when they stumble. According to the program's website, boys who participated in the program improved their grade point averages 57%, reduced their discipline referrals by 79%, and stayed in school.

The mythopoetic men's movement. Since the 1980s, men such as Robert Bly, Michael Meade, Sam Keen, and James Hillman have led a loose collection of organizations active in men's work.

Its mission has been to identify, explain, and celebrate the core of masculinity – both its hard and soft side – with teaching and ritual.

Twenty-first century crusaders. Jackson Katz, a former all-star football player, became the first man at the University of Massachusetts, Amherst to earn a minor in women's studies. After 20 years, his *Mentors in Violence Prevention* (MVP) program has challenged tens of thousands of boys and men across the country at colleges and universities, in youth sports associations, and the military. Roberta Valente of American Bar Association Commission on Domestic Violence lauds "Jackson's dynamic theories and teaching style [that] have had a profound impact... We count on him to open the eyes and ears of lawyers and judges as we try to spread the word that violence against women is everybody's business."

With the power of an evangelist, Katz confronts Caucasian men as a class that rules and sometimes oppresses those in other groups. Because the man-pack has the power to dictate the national conversation, it rarely even perceives itself as domineering, allowing itself to go unexamined, to be invisible.

Katz asserts, however, that the real problem is not malevolent men; it's the bystanders who allow the others to act out. Quoting Martin Luther King, Jr. in his May 2013 TED Talk – "In the end what will hurt the most is not the words of our enemies but the silence of our friends," – Katz contends it's the bystanders who are most open to change and therefore should be most challenged. These are the men who walk idly by in the presence of bullying, domestic violence, sexual assault, or the less lethal, but still damaging, verbal degradation of women in demeaning language and disparaging jokes.

Katz states that the solution is not sensitivity but leadership training for what we call "the great middle of men." He cites the failure of colleges and universities to hold domestic violence and sexual trainings for athletes that stems from an absence of *conscious* governance. He concludes his talk with the invigorating exhortation: "We need more men with the guts, with the courage, with the strength, with the moral integrity, to break our complicit silence, and challenge each other, and stand with women and not against them."

Like Katz, Tony Porter, creator of the advocacy group, *A Call to Men*, sees both the problem and the solution in those he terms "well-meaning men." Porter, who has an large following on YouTube (his TED Talk has more than 1.5 million views), suggests that men are trapped inside a man-box which has traditionally *normalized* domestic violence and sexual assault by socializing men to view women as "less than" men, to see them as property and objects of sexual desire.

Porter throws down the gauntlet to men, saying that they need to examine and challenge their own sexism, stop colluding with other men, get out of their defined roles in society, and take a stance. They must remember that silence is affirming: when men choose not to speak out, they support the behavior.

Lastly, Porter reminds men that "living in the United States of America means sexism is a feature of a larger problem, that we live in a construct that was purposely designed as a race, sex, and class-based system of domination. So, when speaking of ending sexual and domestic violence, we must, men and women both, *accept and own the reality that we are not doing the best work we can until the voices of women of color inform us that we are* [our italics]."

Katz and Porter are only two of a group of courageous men who, in the tradition of suffragettes, crisscross the country – these days by plane rather than coach or train – to preach a message that in its own way promotes human rights as did the suffragettes' campaign a century ago.

With missions that complement the work of Katz and Porter, organizations such as MenEngage and White Ribbon Campaign advance the cause of gender equality at the worldwide level. In its call to action, MenEngage, a global alliance of non-governmental organizations and United Nations' agencies, suggests that men's involvement in creating more gender equality can have significant benefits that include a reduction in poverty, increased education, improvement in overall health, and more peaceful societies. The White Ribbon Campaign, which may be best known for asking men to wear white ribbons as a "pledge to never commit, condone, or remain silent about violence against women and girls," operates in over 60 countries throughout the world. It, too, envisions a masculinity that "embodies the best qualities of being human," and works to challenge negative, outdated concepts of manhood while inspiring men to understand and embrace their potential to be a part of positive change.

The Mankind Project/New Warriors. Offering a globally-recognized and respected men's weekend retreat, the Mankind Project's challenging New Warrior Training Adventure increases self-awareness, teaches accountability, congruence, and affinity with other men. The weekend is followed by peer-facilitated mentoring groups that the website describes as serving over 10,000 men every week. By encouraging work with youth, prisoners, and veterans, the Project helps men discover and live personal missions of service.

Center for the Study of Men and Masculinities. At a time when Centers for Women's Studies have become common at colleges and universities across the country, the John D. and Catherine T. MacArthur Foundation has awarded a multi-year grant to establish the first Center for the Study of Men and Masculinities at Stony Brook University in New York state. The Center's mission is to foster, "a world in which everyone, regardless of race, gender, or sexuality, can reach their full potential as human beings... and furthers the development of boys and men in the service of healthy masculinities and greater gender equality."

Unexpected Allies in Liberating Men

Men such as Porter and Katz, and organizations such as B2M and the Mankind Project, are in the vanguard of change. Not to be ignored are those national institutions and organizations that have their own agendas, but have adopted some ideology and goals associated with men's emancipation. Here are four influential entities in the United States in which the vision of a new masculinity is gaining traction.

Law and order. Law enforcement and criminal justice were initially grounded on the most basic traits of patriarchy: control, retribution, and subjugation. While greatly increasing their emphasis on justice and due-process, until recently the system still faltered when it came to treating women fairly, especially in the arena of domestic violence. Law enforcement failed to make arrests, and prosecutors often dropped charges, until women succeeded in launching battered women's shelters and putting the problem of domestic violence squarely in front of police and the courts. As women found their voices, they articulated their demand that domestic violence no longer be perceived as a "woman's issue" because virtually all the perpetrators were men. When men do the violence, they are the problem.

The standard police response to a man who had battered his wife, which used to be nothing more than a request that the man, sometimes drunk, leave the home for the night, has been replaced with an overnight stay in jail and sometimes a longer jail or prison sentence. Equally significant, probation or parole now includes weekly attendance at tough-minded batterer intervention groups for six to 12 months. The curricula of these groups not only demands accountability, but also requires these men look straight in the mirror at their mascupathic traits: resocializing them to perceive the harm they do and to experience empathy for the pain they cause.

One other remarkable outcome is that, because of women's success in changing how domestic violence is viewed by law enforcement and the courts, men who are victimized by other men or women are now more likely to find support themselves.

In the arena of substance abuse, the testimonies of Mothers Against Drunk Driving and the visionary work of Janet Reno, attorney general in the Clinton administration, overturned thousands of years of judicial procedure with the invention of drug/sobriety courts, now operating or being planned in all 50 states, the District of Columbia, Guam, and Puerto Rico.

Sobriety courts have turned the court system upside down, relying on restorative justice, group consciousness, and a system of rewards as well as traditional punishments. With a focus on the opportunity for rehabilitation rather than retribution, these courts not only result in reduced recidivism but also provide men with new opportunities for self-disclosure, empathy, and an increased sense of community.

Innovative rehabilitation programs are now becoming a part of the criminal justice system. A 2013 article in *Huffington Post* reports that studies show in-prison rehabilitation programs can significantly decrease the probability of re-offence. The article, "Can Theater Help Solve California's Prison Overcrowding Crisis?" concludes that "any successful system of rehabilitation requires multiple components, ranging from mental health and drug treatment to education and skills training." The Actors' Gang Prison Project, initiated by actor and director Tim Robbins, is one such example. Inmates in California's prisons attend an eight-week program, each lasting four hours. As a result, rival prison gang members have developed deep bonds and have transcended race barriers. In the world of treatment, the means of change is termed experiential, and the activities themselves called psychodrama. Robbins and his group are transforming men's psyches.

Veterans Affairs. At the same time the criminal justice system has turned to fairness and rehabilitation, Veterans Affairs have changed the way they address and treat wounded warriors. In World War One, men who showed signs of trauma were deemed "shell-shocked" and lacking in "moral fiber." Even as recently as the war in Viet Nam, tens of thousands of veterans who came home with debilitating wounds and trauma were expected to tough it out like their able-bodied comrades. Thousands suffered alcoholism and drug addiction; many never fully recovered from their experiences. But now, programs such as the Combat Stress Recovery Program (CSRP) are approaching veterans with the sensitivity and affirmation one might associate with a humanistic therapist. On its website, the CSRP shares these crucial four messages with our emotionally-traumatized veterans:

> Here are four important things to know:
>
> - You are not alone.
> - This is not about weakness.
> - You deserve to heal and recover from the invisible, psychological wounds of war as much as you would deserve care for the physical wounds of war.
> - Help is available.

The first two statements overtly reject conventional masculine values isolation and stoicism, implicitly replacing them with relationship and vulnerability. "You are not alone" uses words which recall how empathic adults speak to hurt children. "This is not about weakness" tells veterans that their struggles are legitimate and appropriate: it's okay to be anxious and depressed.

136

The last two statements give the traumatized veteran the comfort of understanding that, when left untreated, emotional wounds are as painful and debilitating as physical wounds. With a few changes, these statements would be indistinguishable from what we tell men in support groups: "You deserve to heal and recover from the invisible, psychological wounds of your present life as much as you would deserve care for the inevitable wounds of childhood."

The CSRP website also highlights Project Odyssey™, "an outdoor, rehabilitative retreat that promotes peer connection, challenging outdoor experiences, and healing with other combat veterans." In our business, this is usually indoors, and we call it "group therapy."

Corporations. Corporate America is changing what success looks like. Arianna Huffington, president and editor-in-chief of the Huffington Post Media Group, has asserted, "We've all bought into this male definition of success, money and power, and it's not working. It's not working for men, and it's not working for women. It's not working for anyone."

Huffington's 2013 conference, "The Third Metric: Redefining Success Beyond Money & Power," began with the observation that "the two metrics of success that drive the American workplace are money and power, which by themselves, they make a two-legged stool – fine for balancing on for a short time, but after a while, you're headed for a fall. Guided by this limited definition of success, more and more 'successful' people are falling. What's needed is a third leg that consists of wisdom, wonder, and the ability to give back." Huffington's initiatives have led to a new conversation about the meaning of work.

There are also signs the corporate world is becoming less hierarchal and more egalitarian:

- James MacGregor Burns, presidential biographer and political scientist, has termed a model of corporate leadership as "post-heroic"
- A program at Columbia Business School teaches sensitive leadership and social intelligence, including reading of facial expressions and body language

- Michelle Patterson, in an article for *In Business Magazine*, refers to research by the Organization for Economic Cooperation and Development, which shows that more companies are recognizing the value of specific feminine traits that drive motivation and higher productivity. These include a "nurturing attitude, open and ongoing communication, and a collaborative spirit"
- Jamie Ladge, Assistant Professor of Management and Organizational Development at Northeastern University, says, "We never explicitly say, 'Develop your feminine side,' but it's clear that's what we're advocating."

Sports. Mascupathy unchained: grandiosity, intimidation, sometimes violence. Coaches who shame and reprimand seven-year-old boys. Competition that turns ugly, sometimes violent. Winning at any cost; where pride/pay are rewards for physically injuring an opponent.

In his article for the *Wall Street Journal*, "Hard Knocks for America's Game," Mark Yost talks about the excitement of a new football season and then goes on to point out the game's dark side.

> Beyond the glitz, football has a large disreputable, even sordid side. Among professional athletes, the wins and losses are enormous, the prize of being at the top perhaps bigger than any other in society. In such a culture, a distortion of values is almost inevitable. Violence on the field, arrests for sexual assault, domestic abuse, drunk driving.

Among the distortion of values that Yost mentions, there's the catastrophic issue of permanent debilitating head injuries that seems to have not received the attention it deserves from NFL owners. The owners have changed the rules of the game to reduce head injuries, but mainly their interest seems to be the minimization of the problem, and it's the "kachink" of cash registers – $9.2 billion in 2012 – that succeeds in drowning out the cries of injured men.

Jock culture. In 2013, Ritchi Incognito, a Miami Dolphins football player, allegedly threatened rookie Jonathon Martin and his family in voicemails and texts, and used racial and homophobic slurs to belittle Martin until he quit the game he loved. Worse, Incognito's teammates supported his behavior, viewing it as usual and insignificant. Like the big bully on the block who beats up the little kid, the community had further victimized the victim.

Brandon Marshall, star wide receiver for the Chicago Bears, is both one of the most extreme examples of unbridled mascupathy and someone who has nevertheless transformed himself into a vessel of hope for the beleaguered sport. Marshall's life has been an exercise in excess: arrests for domestic violence, assault on a police officer, misdemeanor battery, and driving under the influence of alcohol. He attended counseling but it was several years later that he was finally admitted to McLean's Hospital in Belmont, Massachusetts, an apparent turning point, where he was diagnosed with borderline personality disorder.

Instead of shying away from his diagnosis, Marshall violated the unwritten rules of mascupathy by announcing he had one of the more serious mental illnesses. Beyond that, in a talk before the National Alliance on Mental Illness, Marshall articulated his desire to change: "I'm not a new person; I'm just a better person. I'm going to play with more emotion, but it's going to be productive emotion. And if I mess up, I'm going to be a man and stand up and say I messed up."

Marshall was also one of the few football players to speak out about the Incognito debacle. Referring to Incognito's behavior, he said:

> That's what I mean by the culture of the NFL. And that's what we have to change. So what's going on in Miami goes on in every locker room. But it's time for us to start talking. Maybe have some group sessions where guys sit down and maybe talk about what's going on off the field or what's going on in the building and not mask everything. Because the [longer] it goes untreated, the worse it gets.

Everyday sports. Professional sports are so much larger than life that it's easy to forget other incarnations of American sports: kids' softball games, guys' pick-up basketball, Friday night high school football, and racquetball at the local club. In fact, in terms of participants, recreational and school sports are many times the size of pro sports. And although they're often just a good time, caught in the mayhem of mascupathy and the shadow of professional sports, they can take on some of the worst excess of their glitzy big brother.

The less-than-desirable behavior of many pro sports stars seeps into the psyches of boys at a time when there are few heroes who demonstrate accountability. Why then are we surprised at violence on the court, the rink, or the field, or stories of deadly hazing, under-age drinking at team parties, or the loss of a moral compass and subsequent rape of a schoolmate?

But there's hope: Just as Marshall has become a prophet for changing the bullying culture in pro sports, Joe Ehrmann, a former Syracuse University All-American and NFL star, travels across this nation with a mission to revolutionize coaching in order to change kids' sports and boys themselves. Second only to parents, he says, coaches can impact young people as no one else can. But most coaches fail to do the teaching, the mentoring, or the sometimes life-saving intervention their platforms could offer.

Ehrmann makes the distinction between *transactional* and *transformational* coaches. "The transactional coach focuses on winning and meeting his personal needs. He views sports as a transaction: the athlete performs to a coach's demands and in return gets something, usually praise or a position in the starting lineup. The transformational coach uses his platform to teach the Xs and Os, but also the Ys of life. He helps young people grow into responsible adults; he leaves a lasting legacy."

One of the hopeful signs that a new and broader template for men has emerged is the increased awareness, policies, and programs of these enormously powerful organizations. We have entered a time for men who not only get first downs, but also recognize and speak of their emotional struggles, men who gaze deeply beyond their reflection, and are not afraid to affirm other men. We will know that the paradigm has shifted when unbridled male aggression and violence become anomalies and are no longer "just the way things are."

The Missing Link

Our work as therapists is treatment, but it's more than that. Any therapist who tells you he has no agenda – no particular formula for what constitutes the good and responsible life – either deludes himself or you. Certainly we attempt to keep our agenda within bounds; working primarily to address universal issues with widely acceptable outcomes, and maintaining good boundaries so we don't project our beliefs on our clients. But, as therapists who work with men, beyond treating men's struggles with their masculinity, we join Katz and Porter in advocating for societal change.

In our practices, treatment and societal advocacy often overlap. For example, when we help a raging man gain empathy for the effects of his anger on his wife and children, we also teach him to have a larger compassion, one for the plight of all women in abusive relationships. Framing a man's behavior as a societal problem not only makes our prescriptions more acceptable, but also encourages him to carry the message beyond the confines of his home.

Over many years, we recognized that some men were getting our message on both a personal and macro level, but many were not. Probably few were incorporating it as we might wish. Perhaps they managed their controlling behavior better at home, but on the street, they still referred to women as "bitches." Maybe they stopped cheating on their wives, but they still used pornography. Maybe, even more personally distressing for us, they put on "a great act" in group and never changed at all.

Discovering empathy. We realized that in order for men to truly make progress they needed to learn to empathize with the oppression that women experience. That meant our therapy demanded a new intervention.

We needed to help men discover that, much like women, they themselves were the victims of mascupathy; *just as they were the oppressors, they also were the oppressed.* Regardless of their economic or social class, one moment, the men in our groups could take on the part of the oppressor – a malevolent boss or condescending neighbor and, only moments later, they might find themselves in

141

the role of the oppressed – shamed by a demeaning police officer or humiliated by an angry spouse. The unrecognized frequency with which their roles changed minute by minute, day by day, damaged their psyches and contributed to their general malaise. Most of the men in our groups could sense the discomfort but couldn't name its source. Our job was to bring this secret to the light of day.

We established this missing link – that men themselves are victims of mascupathic oppression – so that they would see that mascupathy has no gender lines; its consequences affect all. If they could perceive their suffering from mascupathy – the callous remark of a friend, the condescending attitude of a car mechanic, their own father's disapproval of their failure to get a promotion – they would have empathy for the suffering they and other men cause. They might even learn the next step: to carry the message to other men.

As our colleague, Al Heystek has repeatedly pointed out, "We've got to get [men] to connect to their pain to understand that mascupathy, not women or the law or even mental illness, is the problem. We've got to get them to feel the oppression of mascupathy and the damage it does to themselves, women, and children. And the way we do that is by getting them to experience the pain of being both subjugates and subjugators."

The Tipping Point

Societal change usually takes place not because of one cataclysmic event but as a result of a confluence. Bottom-line, all of these accounts of change have one theme: balance. Mascupathy is fundamentally a problem of imbalance, the exaggeration of the masculine and minimization of the feminine. It's an imbalance that leads to shooters and ruins relationships. We need men who can be tough in tough situations: war, running down criminals, restoring the power grid after huge storms. But what we need more are men who have found balance, who are also humane, kind, understanding, and connected to other human beings in deep ways.

The hope for loving relationships, healthy families, and safe schools rests in a balance that will come from a decline in

142

mascupathy's prevalence and the growth of men's awareness of themselves and connection to community. It's the sense that defined the transformation of our client, David, a lonely and wounded man, who came out from his hiding place with relief and joy, welcomed by the other guys in the group to a new life.

Reaching that balance is a re-discovery that all men can make – a recollected elation of a boy hoisted over his dad's head – a feeling most have forgotten, but once remembered, an invitation to reclaim the sweetness of the kid they once were.

Epilogue

In December 2013, playwright Eve Ensler interviewed actress and activist Jane Fonda and caught her off-guard when she asked, "What's a burning thing you have on your mind these days?" Fonda responded:

> I have a grandson, who is eight, [and] I think a lot about what do we do about our sons. You know, you read the headlines about Columbine and all the school shootings and the headlines say, 'What's happening to our children?' 'What's happening to America's teenagers?' [But the real question is…] 'What's happening to our sons?'
>
> It goes back to this issue of bifurcation and how we raise our sons or our grandsons… I want to put in a plug for us doing everything we can to keep our sons and grandsons emotionally literate, to keep them connected head to heart… I work with adolescents, and the boys who have remained hooked up are in a not-safe place. They're called sissies and pansies and mama's boys. [The ones that don't stay connected] don't know anymore when they're sad. They don't know why they're doing a lot of what they're doing… like sex and drugs and booze… It's because they're depressed. They lose emotional literacy.

For many, Fonda's message has a strong resonance. As a species, our great hope has always been our young. And yet, sometimes intentionally, and other times unwittingly, we raise our boys to lose their emotionality and connection with others, to taunt and bully, and, becoming lonely and depressed, to act out like their fathers and forefathers.

But even those parents who consciously set out to raise their sons in a different way may still feel conflicted. Cheryl L. Erwin, author of *The Everything Parent's Guide to Raising Boys: A Complete*

145

> In an age of women's liberation and political correctness ... parents have been encouraged to avoid gender bias and ... [are] discouraged from teaching stereotypes to their sons and daughters. Little girls should not be restricted to dolls, this reasoning went; instead, they should be encouraged to become police officers and doctors, not 'just mommies.'

Erwin points out those parents of little boys face a more difficult challenge.

> The same parent who chuckles as his son tumbles around the playground, shaking his head and saying with a smile, 'Boys will be boys,' may feel a small stab of worry when that same little boy picks up his sister's doll and contentedly settles down to play.

Randy Flood, co-author of this book, considers himself an emancipated parent. But, probably like many fathers, there have been times when he found himself dismayed by his son's choices.

> *Growing up, Zach played baseball, basketball, football, and piano. He sang in choir and performed in church musicals. I got him private pitching and batting lessons, enrolled him in basketball and football camps. He excelled in all three sports, at the same time demonstrating talent in non-athletic "side" projects.*
>
> *In his sophomore year of high school, Zach quit baseball to audition for the school musical. "Why quit baseball?" I mused. "Baseball is a less violent sport for thinking men. I played baseball, your uncles played baseball, your grandfathers played baseball!" Zach said he wanted more balance in his life. I supported his decision but was secretly disappointed.*
>
> *Then, in his junior year, Zach quit basketball to focus on drama and it felt like a wallop when he summarily announced he was going to sing instead of swing, dance instead of shoot hoops. What was next to go? Football?*
>
> *To my relief, Zach remained committed to the gridiron his senior year. Once again, his team made it to the state championship. Zach caught a touchdown pass in the third of five overtimes,*

helping his team win back-to-back championships. He had lived out the most heroic of masculine fantasies. I was elated and proud. That same year, Zach's goal – to get a lead in the school musical – was realized: he was cast as Ozzie, the sailor in On the Town.

It had been disturbing to me – considering myself to be an enlightened man and realizing that I was hanging on to the need for an alpha son, an arrangement lauded in the man-pack. Zach embodied what I thought in my head and helped me realize it in my heart as well.

In their book, *Raising Cain*, Dan Kindlon and Michael Thompson tell the story of Thompson's "aha moment" with his son, Will. During a severe thunderstorm, Will was clearly frightened. After the storm, Thompson considered several options in talking with his son. One was the culturally-stereotyped response encouraging the boy to be tough: "You weren't scared, were you, buddy?" Instead, Thompson asked, "That was a little scary, wasn't it, Will?" Will's reply? "Dad, that was a *lot* scary."

Both Flood and Thompson are sensitive to their sons in their own ways. Zach and Will, in turn, "demonstrate a growing inner wisdom" that Niobe Way says is found in most boys. Way, a developmental psychologist and author of the best-selling book *Deep Secrets: Boys' Friendships and the Crisis of Connection*, suggests that beyond sensitivity it *is* "in boys' nature to want connection and emotional support." This is how a 15-year-old boy describes this need to Way:

> My ideal best friend is a close, close friend who I could say anything to…cause sometimes you need to spill your heart out to somebody and if there's nobody there, then you gonna keep it inside, then you will have anger. So you need somebody to talk to always.

Unfortunately, as Way followed these boys into adolescence, she discovered a disturbing trend. Even before they entered high school, they were pummeled by the recurring messages of mascupathy to deny the need for authentic relationships into their adult lives and pushed to live in the corrosive belief that they could *go it alone.* Way concludes, *"The problem doesn't lie with the boys themselves but with our constructions of boyhood, manhood."*

Hope from a small town. Here's the touching story of adolescent boys from the small town of Olivet, Michigan who, in contrast to Way's research, still maintained their inner wisdom and a strong desire for inclusion and connection.

In the "On the Road" segment for CBS Evening News, Steve Hartman reported that the Olivet Middle School football team concocted a couple of plays that weren't in the playbook. In the first, to everyone's surprise, the running back took a dive one yard short of the goal line. In the second, the team brought in a new ball carrier, Keith Orr, an unpopular boy who struggled with learning disabilities, to score the touchdown. Hartman concluded his account for "On the Road" by pointing out that the change in Olivet Middle School may make Orr's touchdown "the most successful football play of all time."

What's significant here is not just the admirable rejection of bullying the "weird" kid, the sacrificing of personal gain in scoring a touchdown, or even the love expressed by middle school boys for someone who's "different." As we consider the raising of boys, what's impressive is the number of hits the YouTube video of the story has received: at the time of this writing – over five million. Maybe it's a sign that people are looking for something more than competition and success from boys; that they want to see boys' tenderness last into adolescence and adulthood.

When Arianna Huffington told the attendees at the 2013 Third Metric conference that success needed to be redefined beyond money and power, she listed precisely the same qualities that the boys of Olivet exhibited and millions of people praised: "wisdom, wonder, and the ability to give back."

We know it takes a village to raise a child; perhaps the message of the response to the Olivet story is that our national village has broadened its consciousness of what boys and men need: conventional success, of course, but more – wisdom, wonder, and a sense of belonging to the larger community.

Resources

Ackerman, Diane. *A Slender Thread: Rediscovering Hope at the Heart of Crisis.* New York: Vintage, 1998.

Betcher, R. William., and William S. Pollack. *In a Time of Fallen Heroes: The Re-creation of Masculinity.* New York: Atheneum, 1993.

Bradshaw, John. *Healing the Shame That Binds You.* Deerfield Beach, FL: Health Communications, 2005.

Brooks, Gary R. *Beyond the Crisis of Masculinity: A Transtheoretical Model for Male-friendly Therapy.* Washington, DC: American Psychological Association, 2010.

Brown, Brene. *Daring Greatly: How the Courage to Be Vulnerable Transforms the Way We Live, Love, Parent, and Lead.* New York, NY: Gotham, 2012.

Connell, R.W. *The Men and the Boys.* Hoboken: Wiley, 2013.

Courtenay, Will H. *Dying to Be Men: Psychosocial, Environmental, and Biobehavioral Directions in Promoting the Health of Men and Boys.* New York: Routledge, 2011.

Dutton, Donald, and Susan Golant. *The Batterer: a Psychological Profile.* New York: Basic Books, 2008.

Ehrmann, Joe, Paula Ehrmann, and Gregory Jordan. *InSideOut Coaching: How Sports Can Transform Lives.* New York, NY: Simon & Schuster, 2011.

Friedan, Betty. *The Feminine Mystique.* New York: Norton, 2001.

Garbarino, James. *Lost Boys: Why Our Sons Turn Violent and How We Can Save Them.* New York: Anchor, 2000.

Ghiglieri, Michael Patrick. *The Dark Side of Man: Tracing the Origins of Male Violence.* Reading, MA: Perseus, 2000.

Gilbert, Paul, and Bernice Andrews. *Shame: Interpersonal Behavior, Psychopathology, and Culture.* New York: Oxford University Press, 1998.

Gilligan, James. *Violence: Reflections on a National Epidemic.* New York: Vintage, 1996.

Gilligan, Carol. *In a Different Voice: Psychological Theory and Women's Development.* Cambridge, MA: Harvard University Press, 2001.

Goleman, Daniel. *Emotional Intelligence.* 10th anniversary pb. ed. New York: Bantam Books, 2005.

Helgeson, Vicki S. *The Psychology of Gender.* 4th ed. Boston: Pearson, 2012.

Johnson, Allan G. *The Gender Knot: Unraveling our Patriarchal Legacy.* Revised and updated ed. Philadelphia, PA: Temple University Press, 2005.

Katz, Jackson. *The Macho Paradox: Why Some Men Hurt Women and How All Men Can Help.* Naperville, IL.: Sourcebooks, Inc., 2006.

Katz, Jackson. *Leading Men: Presidential Campaigns and the Politics of Manhood.* Northampton, MA: Interlink Books, 2013.

Kimmel, Michael S. *Angry White Men: American Masculinity at the End of an Era.* New York: Nation Books, 2013.

Kimmel, Michael S. *The Gendered Society.* New York: Oxford University Press, 2000.

Kindlon, Daniel J., Michael Thompson, and Teresa Barker. *Raising Cain: Protecting the Emotional Life of Boys.* New York: Ballantine, 1999.

Kivel, Paul. *Men's Work: How to Stop the Violence That Tears Our Lives Apart.* Center City, MN: Hazelden, 1992.

Kupers, Terry Allen. *Revisioning Men's Lives: Gender, Intimacy, and Power.* New York: Guilford, 1993.

Lee, John H. *The Flying Boy: Healing the Wounded Man.* FL: Health Communications, Inc., 1991.

Lee, John H. *The Half-lived Life: Overcoming Passivity and Rediscovering Your Authentic Self.* Guilford, CT: Lyons, 2012.

Lerner, Harriet. *The Dance of Intimacy: A Woman's Guide to Courageous Acts of Change in Key Relationships.* New York, NY: Harper & Row, 1989.

Lerner, Harriet. *The Dance of Connection: How to Talk to Someone When You're Mad, Hurt, Scared, Frustrated, Insulted, Betrayed, or Desperate.* New York: Quill, 2002.

Levant, Ronald F., and Gary R. Brooks. *Men and Sex: New Psychological Perspectives.* New York: J. Wiley, 1997.

Levant, Ronald F., and Gini Kopecky. *Masculinity Reconstructed: Changing the Rules of Manhood - At Work, in Relationships, and in Family Life.* New York N.Y.: Dutton, 1995.

Bar-Levav, Reuven. *Thinking in the Shadow of Feelings: A New Understanding of the Hidden Forces That Shape Individuals and Societies.* New York: Simon and Schuster, 1988.

Lewis, Helen Block. *Shame and Guilt in Neurosis.* New York: International Universities, 1971.

Okun, Rob A. *Voice Male: The Untold Story of the Profeminist Men's Movement.* Northampton, MA: Interlink Publishing Group, 2014.

Osherson, Samuel. *Finding Our Fathers: How a Man's Life Is Shaped by His Relationship with His Father.* New York: Fawcett Columbine, 1987.

Pence, Ellen, Michael Paymar, Tineke Ritmeester, and Melanie Shepard. *Education Groups for Men Who Batter: The Duluth Model.* New York: Springer Publishing, 1993.

Pennebaker, James W. *Emotion, Disclosure & Health.* 2nd ed. Washington, DC: American Psychological Association, 1997.

Pittman, Frank S. *Man Enough: Fathers, Sons, and the Search for Masculinity.* New York: G.P. Putnam's Sons, 1993.

Pleck, Joseph H. *The Myth of Masculinity.* Cambridge, MA: MIT, 1983.

Pollack, William S. *Real Boys: Rescuing Our Sons from the Myths of Boyhood*. New York: Random House, 1998.

Pollack, William S., and Ronald F. Levant. *New Psychotherapy for Men*. New York: J. Wiley, 1998.

Real, Terrence. *I Don't Want to Talk about It: Overcoming the Secret Legacy of Male Depression*. New York: Fireside, 1998.

Rosen, David. *The Changing Fictions of Masculinity*. Urbana: University of Illinois, 1993.

Rosin, Hanna. *The End of Men: And the Rise of Women*. London: Penguin, 2013.

Sax, Leonard. *Why Gender Matters: What Parents and Teachers Need to Know about the Emerging Science of Sex Differences*. New York: Doubleday, 2005.

Schnarch, David Morris. *Intimacy & Desire: Awaken the Passion in Your Relationship*. New York, NY: Beaufort, 2009.

Way, Niobe. *Deep Secrets: Boys, Friendships, and the Crisis of Connection*. London: Harvard University Press, 2013.

Wexler, David B. *When Good Men Behave Badly: Change Your Behavior, Change Your Relationship*. Oakland, CA: New Harbinger Publications, 2004.

Wiseman, Rosalind. *Masterminds & Wingmen: Helping Our Boys Cope with Schoolyard Power, Locker-room Tests, Girlfriends, and the New Rules of Boy World*. New York: Harmony, 2013.

Acknowledgements

We've learned about men from university professors, writers in our field, insightful and wise colleagues, and from our own therapy. But we learned most from the struggling guys in our therapy rooms who muster the courage to look themselves in the mirror and free their hearts to create authentic selves and strong relationships. They deserve our deepest gratitude.

In addition to the men we've worked with, we're grateful to those who worked with us. Many of our observations came from our personal journeys beneath our masculinity's armor. Sometimes invigorating and always challenging, our therapists and mentors have stayed with us over many years: John Weiks, Nancy Jonker, Kirk Brink, Sally Ryan, Natan Harpaz, David Mutchler, Seamus Norguaard, I Wayan Sukarta, Jeff & Kit Crawford, David & Julie Bernstein, colleagues in the supervision group, and the steadfast and visionary men in our personal men's groups.

We value our professional colleagues: Amy Van Gunst, Al Heystek, Rob Okun, Fanchon Clark, Ken Porter, and interns Chelsea VanTongeren and Chris Roberts. We thank the many readers who read various versions of the manuscript and provided significant feedback. We are grateful for the help from administrative co-workers at the Men's Resource Center of West Michigan: Becky Plantinga and Sandy Berry for keeping us organized, and Raechel Haller for her excellent graphic design and marketing skills. Thanks also to Mike Devarenne for the website, to Sondra Loucks Wilson, who cheerfully pummeled our manuscript into shape, and to our publicist Gardi Wilks, who offered wise counsel with humor and grace about the wide and wicked world of books and publishing.

When we first started writing this book, we thought it would take a few months. In fact, the process lasted far longer. During that time, Randy appreciated the support and patience of his family—

Stephanie, Zach, and Anna. Charlie was grateful for the understanding of folks who agreed not to call him during his early morning prime writing time.

Occasionally, our family and friends challenged us: "All you guys do is work on this damn book. Don't you think you're pretty mascupathic yourselves?" We smiled, mildly chagrined, and thanked them, knowing we still had our own personal work to do.

About the Authors

Charlie Donaldson's passion is the exploration of the human psyche, which first led him to the world of literature, particularly the novels of Fitzgerald and Joyce. After teaching college English for many years, he found a new venue for his explorations as a counseling psychologist. Donaldson's mission is to create environments in which men, including himself, can grow into the naturally big-hearted people they really are. He has Master's degrees in English from Wayne State University and in Counseling Psychology from Western Michigan University. He is credentialed as a Limited Licensed Psychologist and Licensed Professional Counselor.

In addition to personal and clinical work, Donaldson has co-authored *Stop Hurting the Woman You Love: Breaking the Cycle of Abusive Behavior* (Hazelden, 2006); written *Restorative Treatment: A New Specialty in Counseling;* and the *Smart and Effective* series of manuals for treatment of substance abuse, domestic violence, and other men's issues.

Since retiring, Donaldson divides his time between his homes on Beaver Island and in Petoskey, Michigan, both which overlook the shores of Lake Michigan and provide ideal settings for reflection and writing. He's grateful for a loving community of men and women who seek liberation for both genders, and for his dog, Benny, a spiritual guide whose boundless enthusiasm provides him daily lessons of the joy of living in the present.

*   *   *   *   *   *   *

Randy Flood is a Limited Licensed Psychologist and director of the Men's Resource Center of West Michigan where he has developed gender-specific approaches to therapy with men, and created targeted clinical services that address issues of male identity, trauma, emotional illiteracy, inadequate relationship skills, and addiction. Often called upon as an expert witness for district and circuit courts, he also provides trainings on problems such as bullying, domestic violence, sexual addiction, and men in counseling.

A contributing author to Rob Okun's book, *VOICE MALE: The Untold Story of the Profeminist Men's Movement* (Interlink Books), and co-author of *Stop Hurting the Woman You Love: Breaking the Cycle of Abusive Behavior* (Hazelden, 2006), Flood writes for *Voice Male* magazine and other publications as well as acting as media consultant on men's issues.

Flood lives in Grand Rapids, Michigan with his wife, Stephanie, with whom he loves to travel. He relishes reading and photography, as well as playing percussion and softball. In addition, he enjoys the challenge of competing in triathlons. His greatest accomplishment and joy over the years has been being a father to his two adult children, Anna and Zach.

*   *   *   *   *   *   *

Charlie Donaldson and Randy Flood see themselves not only as therapists but as advocates. More than an explanation of distorted masculinity and its treatment, this book is a call to action. In order to facilitate understanding and promote healing, Donaldson and Flood founded and serve as co-directors of the Institute for the Prevention and Treatment of Mascupathy. **www.mascupathy.org**